A FINE ANGER

A FINE ANGER

NEIL PHILIP

*A critical introduction
to the work of*

*Alan
Garner*

PHILOMEL BOOKS

Library of Congress Cataloging in Publication Data

Philip, Neil.   A fine anger.

"Part of a Ph.D. thesis ... accepted by the
University of London in 1980"—Pref.
    Bibliography: p.
    Includes index.
    Summary: A discussion of the works of author
Alan Garner.
    1. Garner, Alan—Criticism and interpretation.
[1. Garner, Alan—Criticism and interpretation.
2. Authors—English] I. Title.
PR6057.A66Z83   1981   823'.914   81-8654
ISBN 0-399-20828-3   AACR2

First published in the United States of America 1981
by Philomel Books, a division of The Putnam Publishing Group,
200 Madison Avenue, New York, N.Y. 10016.
Published in Great Britain by William Collins Sons & Co., Ltd.
Printed in the United States.

Contents

Preface

Everything Alan Garner has published has been published for children.

This simple fact has seriously distorted criticism of Garner's work; I will not, except in this preface, be much concerned with it. This book is about Alan Garner the writer, not Alan Garner the children's writer. I have written it because Garner seems to me to be a very considerable talent, whatever his readership; he is a craftsman in prose, and a distinguished and distinctive one. This contention can only be proved by subjecting his work to the sort of scrutiny one would accord John Fowles, Angus Wilson or B. S. Johnson. Criticism by reference to the needs and reactions of a particular audience can only establish standards inside a genre, and will inevitably be of least use in the most interesting cases. Conversely, whether our admiration for a given children's book is diminished or confirmed by stringent critical enquiry, something will have been learnt in the process. My concern, therefore, will be with the words on the page, and with the space between the words. Only when the quality of the words is established does the nature of their audience become more than a matter for parochial concern.

This does not deny Garner his young audience. It seems clear, from surveys, from the reports of teachers, and from Alan Garner's readers' letters, that children and adolescents do appreciate his work; that, in some cases, the connection between writer and reader is made more forcefully, more directly, more subtly, when the reader is pre-adult. It is equally clear that adults are by no means debarred from enjoying and appreciating Garner's writing: the literary prizes

7

he has won were awarded by adults, though on behalf of children; his reputation among adults not deterred by the 'children's' label stands high.

It may be that Garner's is a case in which the categories of children's and adult literature are meaningless, that his work is enjoyed by a type of person, no matter what their age. It may be that the apparent suitability of his work, for instance the *Stone Book* quartet, for children is a by-product of the refining, condensing, simplifying processes by which he clarifies and makes potent his vision, not their spur.

The first two novels, certainly, were intended as children's books, and they suffer from their obedience to the conventions of the children's fiction of the time. Post-*Elidor*, when Garner is clearly tapping the energy which powers his work at the root, it is difficult to imagine that the author catered for any audience but himself; though in the foreseeing of such an audience lies the impulse to fashion a public rather than a private statement.

Garner's own reactions to questions of audience and intent have been contradictory, and only mildly helpful. The out-of-context quotation on the dust-jacket of *Red Shift* that to express himself in a children's book involves 'subjecting myself to the poetic disciplines – pace, compression, simplicity. That's why I go on writing for children. It's not a minor form. It's a superb discipline which makes me write a better book'[1] may be true, but it does nothing to make *Red Shift* any more or less a children's book. He has denied writing with children in mind, and has also affirmed it.

It is possible that the note of maturity and acceptance in the *Stone Book* quartet signals the conclusion of Garner's career as a children's writer. The quartet effectively resolves the tensions of the preceding books, and I cannot imagine that the books which will follow it will be recognisably children's books, though they may be accessible to children in much the same way as the work published so far is accessible to adults.

It seems best simply to leave the books to be enjoyed by those who enjoy them, adults or children, and to judge them on their purely literary qualities. Educationalists and psychologists may then draw what conclusions they wish as to the books' suitability for a young audience.

8

Garner has often appeared, particularly to adult readers, a complex, difficult, demanding author; critics intent on hunting esoteric meanings and obscure facts have seemed to reduce the books to the level of literary crossword puzzle or parlour game, denying, decrying or ignoring their immediate, accessible qualities. The essence of his work seems to me to be the struggle to render the complex in simple, bare terms; to couch the abstract in the concrete and communicate it directly to the reader. A mode of criticism which ignores this and seeks to demolish the simple statement in search of the complex patterns behind it seems both perverse and self-defeating.

For all that, examination of the processes by which an author has achieved, or has tried to achieve, his ends, and the ways in which he has combined disparate materials to make a whole, can lead to a greater understanding of that whole, and I have tried to indicate sources, influences and parallels where these may be helpful. I hope I have maintained a reasonable balance between surface and background, and have not allowed research to inhibit response.

Alan Garner's writing is intensely autobiographical, in both obvious and subtle ways, but the books need no extraneous biographical information for their full appreciation. In the introduction I give a brief biography, and a general guide to Garner's career. The chapters that follow deal with Garner's works in chronological order. The bibliography is as full as possible: I have tried to include all Garner's published work, all the important critical and biographical writing on him, and a full selection of background reading.

I owe many debts of gratitude both to individuals and to organisations who have helped in the writing of this book in numerous ways. To the Department of Education and Science, and through them the British public, who funded the research on which the book is based, as part of a Ph.D. thesis presented to, and accepted by, the University of London in 1980. To Dr J. S. Bratton, of Bedford College, London University, who oversaw my post-graduate work and made a number of helpful comments. To Linda Davis of Collins, who commissioned this work on the strength of a somewhat scrappy draft of a chapter of my thesis, and to all the staff at Collins. To my parents, and to many friends, most notably Peter and Sylvia

9

Bradford and Brian Hinton, who encouraged me and helped me clarify my ideas; to Chris Neilan, who told me to read the books in the first place; and to Alan and Griselda Garner, who allowed me to intrude upon their privacy and their time. Alan Garner most generously gave me access to his files and manuscripts.

I would also like to thank Jane Alderson, Paddy Bechely, Malcolm Brown, Michael Croucher, Doris Dwight, Mike Healey, Trevor Hill, Diana Reed, Audrey Robins, Herbert Smith and all the others who have helped me hear or see Alan Garner's radio and television work. My gratitude, too, to the many authors living and dead on whose work I have drawn, and especially to those I have quoted.

My greatest debt is to Emma Bradford, and this book is dedicated to her, with love.

NEIL PHILIP
Holland Park, June 1980.

Introduction

Alan Garner was born in his grandmother's front room in Congleton, Cheshire, on 17 October 1934. It was a rare venture off home territory. In practice the physical, emotional and spiritual limits of his childhood were prescribed by the bounds of Alderley Edge, the Cheshire village which has remained central to his writing and his life. His father's family had lived and worked there for generations, in a cottage at the foot of the Edge itself, a dramatic wooded escarpment rising out of the Cheshire plain. The Edge's holy well emerges in their back garden.

Alderley Edge was already, as it appears in *Elidor*, a suburb of Manchester, but for Garner it was a village. It was where he, and his family, belonged, though his clumsiness with his hands ran counter to the family tradition, and distressed both him and his craftsman relations. He went, in the intervals between a succession of severe illnesses, to the village school. He was beaten for speaking dialect, encouraged for being clever, and entered for Manchester Grammar School.

M.G.S., perhaps the most intellectually demanding secondary school in Britain, was a profoundly disorientating experience. It gave Garner's mind the stimulus it needed, and at the same time cut the ground from beneath his feet. Home and school were two worlds, two ways of thinking, two ways of speaking, and they did not marry. The whole of his work has been an exploration of this division and, latterly, an attempt to put the world, the thought and the language of school at the service of those of home. Garner was not a writer at school, but a champion sprinter. He was possessed by the urge to excel.

National Service in the Royal Artillery followed, and Garner found himself responsible for and to men many years his senior, of all backgrounds and types. Though student acting was fun, the study of the classics at Magdalen College, Oxford, seemed a rarefied, inbred, unhealthy activity after that, and Garner was already burning to be doing. He had read William Golding's *The Lord of the Flies* and found his vocation. He was going to be a writer.[1]

He left Oxford without taking his degree, and returned to Cheshire. Eight miles from Alderley he found the workplace he needed, 'a medieval timber-framed house on a site that has almost certainly been occupied by the living for 3,500 years, and by the dead for a good 500 years before that'.[2]

On the afternoon of Tuesday, 4 September 1956, he wrote the first words of the first draft of a magic fantasy novel for children, *The Weirdstone of Brisingamen*. It was subtitled *A Tale of Alderley*, and it took nearly two years to write. Collins accepted it, and it was published in October 1960.

The Weirdstone was an immediate critical success: reviewers, much to their credit, recognised a new voice. The flaws of this book and its successor, the subservience to convention, the inflation of plot and language, have become more apparent over the years as Garner's writing has matured. What was evident then, and still is now, was the books' power, their ebullience, the grand scale on which they worked, their energy. What's more the energy was clearly rooted, secure. It was not conjured from some airy inspiration, but drawn from the rock, soil and sky of Cheshire.

The book's child protagonists, Colin and Susan, are sent to stay with their mother's old nurse and her farmer husband in Alderley. Explorations on the Edge involve them in a gripping tale of magic and fear. The book is essentially a long series of flights and pursuits, with a battle at the climax. Colin and Susan should have expected no less. For beneath the Edge, as Garner's grandfather had told him, one hundred and forty

12

knights lie asleep, and one hundred and forty white horses beside them. A wizard guards them, and the entrance to their cave, for those brave or foolhardy enough to try it, lies through the rocks known as the Iron Gates. They will wake to save the world.

Colin and Susan must stop them being woken too soon. The key to the magic which keeps them asleep is the weirdstone of the title, stolen from the cave by the farmer who in the legend of 'The Wizard of Alderley Edge' supplies the last of the white horses, and brought back to its home as a bracelet on Susan's wrist. It is twice stolen, twice recovered.

The hectic pace is deliberate. Interviewed in 1962 Garner said of the first two books that he wished 'to make every page contain something which is pure excitement and horror, giving the story the tempo of a thriller'.[3] *The Moon of Gomrath*, the sequel, represented an artistic advance but provided a less satisfying story. In the first half of the book Susan is possessed by a shapeless evil, from which Colin must free her; in the second half Colin himself is made prisoner, and Susan must free him. The same witch, the Morrigan, is the enemy again. This time her motive is simply malice and revenge: the game is not played for the same high stakes but the writing is tighter, the characters more lively, the imagery more coherent, and the sense of place just as vivid.

The importance of place to these two books cannot be overemphasised. Alderley is not simply the setting: it *shapes* the stories. To drive or walk around the area is to be inside the books. 'This is where the Morrigan stopped her car'; 'This is where the svarts appeared'; 'This is where Colin and Susan saw the crow'; here are the Iron Gates, Seven Firs, Stormy Point, Saddle Bole, the Goldenstone. The Goldenstone, a massive lump of sandstone riven down the middle by some unknown agency (the Morrigan, readers of *The Moon of Gomrath* would stoutly maintain), was located and uncovered by Garner in the course of local researches which fuelled *The Weirdstone*. Beneath it, he found the polished stone axe which provides the central image of his fifth and most ambitious full-length novel, *Red Shift*.

The local researches have been carried on ever since. Garner's knowledge of the area's history, pre-history, geology and geography is minute, but it is a creative knowledge, not an antiquarian one. For him, the past is still alive, and so is the future. From one window of his study one can see a headless cross like the one at which Durathror makes his desperate last stand in *The Weirdstone of Brisingamen*; from the others, the Jodrell Bank radio telescope. By the side runs a railway line, and the house vibrates as trains go by.

Neither a sense of place nor a sense of the living presence of the past make a great novelist. They are the context in which he can see people: the context which defines what people are. Garner's first two books are all context, and the people whom that context should define are blanks.

In 1962 Garner began to fill in the blanks, with a radio play called *Elidor*. The play was the rather muddled beginning of a third novel, also called *Elidor*, in which dialogue plays a large role, and in which the sound of the human voice seems to have provided Garner with the means to put on paper something of the human heart and mind. Of the four children who are summoned from our world to a wasteland called Elidor and sent one by one by a ruthless warrior king into a burial mound to rescue three 'Treasures', symbols of power from Celtic myth, only the youngest, Roland, the one who succeeds, is fully drawn. Though the other three spring intermittently to life they have little real existence outside their relationship to Roland, whose febrile, high-strung intensity is very sharply and accurately conveyed. It is our sense of Roland as a distinct character which leaves the reader merely thoughtful and perplexed at the end of the story and not entirely baffled, for it is a book which is wrapped in mystery.

The settings, Manchester, Elidor (not entirely an imaginary place; the forest of Mondrum was in Cheshire) and Alderley (the house to which the children move is the one in which Garner was brought up) are again realised in great detail, and with the, albeit fitful, skill in depicting character has come an ability to observe, record and communicate the peculiarities of perception. To place, then, is added character and

14

psychological atmosphere. What is never clarified is theme. The meaning of Elidor, of the Treasures, of the death of the unicorn Findhorn, careering through the streets of Manchester, of Roland's final exclamation of pain is profoundly ambiguous, in a way in which I, at least, found unsettling. The various elements of the ending seem at odds with each other, and it is possible to view the book, easily the most powerful thing Garner had written up to that point, as ending either in a kind of bitter joy or in black despair. It was perhaps inevitable that the transition from the simple excitements of the first two books to the complex emotional interplay of *The Owl Service* should not be accomplished without some confusion or unease.

Garner had had the idea for *The Owl Service*, the book with which he achieved his earlier promise, even before he wrote *Elidor*. A friend had shown him a dinner service with a strange pattern which could be arranged to make pictures of either owls or flowers, and Garner at once associated the plates with the story of Lleu Llaw Gyffes, Blodeuwedd and Gronw Pebyr in the medieval collection of Welsh romances *The Mabinogion*. It is a story of love and jealousy, and at its close Blodeuwedd, the girl who has been made from flowers to be Lleu's wife and then taken Gronw for a lover, is turned into an owl, the bird that all other birds hate. In this story, Garner found a structure to express in contemporary terms something very deeply felt about the timelessness of human emotion and the stifling oppression of possessive love. His story of three teenagers in a Welsh valley whose personal tensions are given shape and terror by the still potent echo of the *Mabinogion* story seems to many the most accomplished, daring and successful children's book for many years. It won the Library Association Carnegie Medal and the *Guardian* Award, and it also started the controversy as to whether Garner was really a children's writer. Many people seemed to feel that *The Owl Service* was simply too good to be a children's book. Beside the pale, enervated, self-regarding, directionless contemporary adult novel it seemed almost insultingly assured, a triumph of compressed thought and feeling. It is this concentration of meaning, and the ability which goes with it to imply whole areas of unstated action and emotion, which remains Garner's most distinctive quality.

The next novel, *Red Shift*, took another six years to write, and carried the compressing process further. In it Garner found the courage to sever conventional narrative links, and to work on a more submerged, organic level. The three interwoven love stories, set in the present day, the English Civil War and the second century A.D., are connected thematically, geographically, symbolically, and most importantly by language and image. It is a complex book but not a complicated one: the bare lines of story and emotion stand clear. Its disregard for a causal, sequential notion of time, which some readers find alarming, is simply a more coherent statement of the view of time which informs all Garner's previous work. The children in *Elidor* are taken outside time for their moment of trial, like the heroes of Garner's later opera libretto *Potter Thompson* and TV play *To Kill a King*; at crucial moments in the first two books time is denied as it is in dreams; *The Owl Service*'s triple structure extends back in time to a still active mythical past. Time is Garner's most consistent theme, and at the root of all his thinking about it lies the idea that what is important of human life endures, and does not decay. It is this which prevents the endings of *The Owl Service* and *Red Shift* from being despairing or depressing, and it is this which is brought out with great clarity in Garner's most important work to date, the *Stone Book* quartet.

The four novellas which make up the quartet, *The Stone Book, Granny Reardun, The Aimer Gate* and *Tom Fobble's Day*, are the calm after the storm of *Red Shift*. Garner had won through to a complete command of the material he had been working and reworking from the start of his career. It is unsurprising that he should then apply himself directly to the question of his family, his culture and his heritage. The first five novels are a slow and painful reknitting of the bonds severed by Manchester Grammar School and Oxford. The quartet celebrates that mending.

Each book centres round a day in the life of a child in four generations of Garners, and their discovery of not simply continuity but contemporaneity with their forebears. Though the books recreate a culture and a life which is now almost entirely gone they are in no sense a valediction. They are a revelation: of a level of English rural life, and of historical awareness, which has not been captured in the novel before. They are something entirely new, and special, and they are the logical outcome of all Garner's previous writing. Though each step is unpredictable it is also inevitable; each book builds on the last, and there is a chain of words, themes, images, thought and technique leading unbroken back to *The Weirdstone of Brisingamen.*

The *Stone Book* quartet marks a watershed in Garner's writing career, and provides a suitable moment for an evaluation of his work so far. He has written little, and the first three of his books, despite their wide popularity and undoubted virtues, have some fairly evident flaws, but his work has been important not only to the development of the children's novel, where he has been widely influential, but also in the context of English literature as a whole.

Garner has never been an author to be catalogued by a listing of literary influences. It is the oral tradition which has fascinated him throughout his career, and the work he has done researching, compiling and retelling folktales has had a profound effect on his writing style. One might sometimes imagine that he lived on the BBC's desert island, with only the Bible, Shakespeare, perhaps the works of the fourteenth-century Gawain poet, and a well-stocked reference library. The Authorised Version is the bedrock of English speech, and Shakespeare of English literature, and no writer can escape from them; the Gawain poet is a touchstone for Garner's use of language, for his success or failure in serving in words the area from which they both come. Any other literary influences or allusions, whether from the classics or comics, are superfluous: the direct, physical, craftsmanly life which Garner celebrates in the *Stone Book* quartet resists literary flourishes. One of the reasons why the books are so short is that every word which is not entirely necessary has been jettisoned. Just as *Red Shift* discarded much of the conventional clutter of 'he said, she said, and then he, and meanwhile she', so in the quartet Garner's prose approaches the texture of poetry. His words are absolutes. There is no qualification, no hesitation, only the clean edge of necessary speech.

This said, Garner is clearly not alone in the English literary tradition. Other contemporary writers have worked in parallel lines, and while our reading of Fielding or Dickens may add nothing to our appreciation of Garner there are comparisons with past writers which it is helpful to make. Garner's work seem to me to engage with that of the nineteenth-century poet John Clare in particularly fruitful ways. The two men share a pride, an obduracy, an intensity of purpose. Blighted first love, set in a minutely realised, numinous landscape, is a recurrent theme in both. Though Clare struggled towards education, and Garner has struggled away from it, or rather around or behind it, their attitudes and insights are often surprisingly similar. They are both inspired by place, but they are neither of them content simply to describe. They enter. They are both, like Hopkins, writers about inscape, not landscape.

Garner has a place with Clare and Hopkins; he deserves our attention alongside David Jones, Ted Hughes, Geoffrey Hill, John Heath-Stubbs, Edwin Muir, to name but a few of the twentieth-century poets who have claimed in their verse, as Garner has in his prose, a priestly function. Hill's *Mercian Hymns*, for example, with its triple focus on the historical Offa, the poet himself and the mythical Offa, conceived as a sort of presiding spirit of Mercia, an ectoplasmic thread stretching from Offa to Hill and capable of physical or conceptual manifestation at any moment, records an attitude to the individual's relationship to time, history and heritage exactly comparable to Garner's. What is interesting is that Hill's work, while brilliant, erudite and innovative, is also, though less so in *Mercian Hymns* than elsewhere, obscure and forbidding. Telling stories has forced Garner to be simple and direct; he has had to submit both intellect and intuition to the

18

discipline of narrative. The result has been less obviously weighty than the work of Hill or Hughes, but just as important. The vigour of the oral tradition has been tranfused into the sluggish bloodstream of the modern novel, and new life imparted.

*Many books are written to make people read
the best are written to force them to think*

JOHN CLARE

1

Alan Garner has not simply produced a number of books but a coherent oeuvre, in which every book is a comment on and refinement of its predecessors. The books cross-refer and intertwine, and the same themes, blighted love, isolation, confrontation with the godhead, redemption, recur throughout. In particular, the books are held together by myth, and by an abiding interest in the nature of the mythical.

Garner is one of the most able of the writers who have sought in the last twenty years to explore the disjointed and troubled psychological and emotional landscape of the twentieth century through the symbolism of myth and folklore: myth is used as a diagnostic tool in the examination of contemporary ills. Central to Garner's writing is a concern with patterning, with repetitive cycles of experience, which he has explored by structuring his stories around myths and legends. Although the use of mythology has become less overt in his later work, and the magical trappings of the early books, plundered willy-nilly from whatever source came to hand, have been discarded, myth is still the energy source which powers his writing. The patterns have simply become barer, more essential, until in *Red Shift* it is well-nigh impossible for the reader to discern beneath the complex narrative scheme the story of the ballad 'Tam Lin' on which Garner assures us the book is based.

In the *Stone Book* quartet he has turned from myth and folklore to oral history, the folklore of a family rather than a community, as a structuring tool, but his subject is the folk life which is folklore's *raison d'être*, and his purpose to establish valid signs for a personal sacrament, not to report events. The *Stone Book* quartet may not be overtly concerned with the world of myth, but of all Garner's work it most nearly approaches anthropologist Maya Deren's penetrating definition of myth in her *Divine Horsemen*, 'the facts of the mind made manifest in a fiction of matter'.

Despite this strong sense of the connectedness of the books, of their being part of a cumulative statement, there are compelling reasons for adopting a largely chronological rather than thematic approach to them. Most particularly, Garner's relatively small output has made the gradual maturing of his artistic vision seem dramatic, and enables the reader to chart the development of his thought and technique with great clarity. Each book has been more complex, more substantial, more commanding than the last. To consider the books individually, and in the order in which they appeared, may well make it easier to grasp the whole.

This approach has one disadvantage: because Garner's writing has improved so much over the years, in the early chapters criticism outweighs appreciation. The first three books are prentice work: fascinating for their intermittent brilliance, and for their thematic consistency with the later books, but flawed. Readers of this study who are interested in Garner at his best might prefer to concentrate on chapters 3, 5 and 7.

The first two novels, *The Weirdstone of Brisingamen* and *The Moon of Gomrath*, may be flawed, but they are arguably Garner's most popular books; certainly it is on them that his reputation as a purely children's author rests. There is between them no great gap in either style or achievement. The second is a direct sequel of the first, employing the same characters and giving them somewhat similar adventures. It has become fashionable to condemn Garner's early work, perhaps because of his own dismissive attitude to it. In 1968 he called *The Weirdstone of Brisingamen* 'a fairly bad book', the first drafts of which were 'the usual condescending pap'; in 1970 he announced that it was 'one of the worst books published in the last twenty years . . . technically . . . inept'. These are unbalanced judgements. Although the books are immature, both have an undeniable ability to involve the reader in their stories. They are, whatever their faults, exciting.

The Weirdstone of Brisingamen takes as its starting point 'The Wizard of Alderley Edge', a local legend told to Garner by his grandfather[1]. The legend is of a type particularly well represented in Britain, the stories of a sleeping king and his knights who will wake to save the world from great peril. In it, a wizard buys a horse from a local farmer to make up the required number of horses and repays him with jewels from a great store (the reputation of which in later times has excited rather more interest in the discovery of the underground caverns than the idea of finding the legendary sleepers). The names of the king and the wizard are not mentioned in the legend, and Garner escapes the commonest trap of children's fantasy writing by refusing to name them as Arthur and Merlin, a reticence which seems all the more praiseworthy when we learn that he had so named them to himself as a child. Writing of his childhood in 'The Edge of the Ceiling' he says: 'we accepted that King Arthur lay asleep behind a rock we called the Iron Gates'. The name he chooses for the wizard (the king is never named), Cadellin Silverbrow, has only tenuous Arthurian connections: Cadellin is mentioned in the long list of names by which Culhwch invokes Arthur's aid in the Welsh Arthurian romance 'Culhwch and Olwen'.

The plot of *The Weirdstone* is a simple framework for exciting adventure, and concerns the fight for the possession of the jewel of the title, which is the key to the magic which keeps the sleepers from waking or growing old. The stone was surreptitiously removed by the farmer of the legend, and ever since the powers of good and evil have been searching for it. Two children, Colin and Susan, are drawn into the world of magic by Susan's unwitting possession of the weirdstone.

The 'eternal fight between good and evil' is a commonplace and overworked theme in fantasy writing, and one that after *The Moon of Gomrath* Garner scrupulously avoids. However, *The Weirdstone of Brisingamen* has four outstanding virtues to compensate for the triteness of its central premise and for the lack of characterisation which is its most serious flaw. Firstly, the book is gripping and enthralling. The story is unstructured, a mere succession of adventures leading to a grand climax, but it holds the attention and keeps the reader guessing what is going to happen next. I suspect that in both *The Weirdstone* and its sequel Garner was seeking to emulate the structural effects he found in the Celtic stories which also supplied him with a language and a frame of reference, and that criticism of the books' structure should bear in mind his comment prefacing 'The Voyage of Maelduin' in *The Hamish Hamilton Book of Goblins*: 'the stories often appear to be strung together at random – and yet there is always the feeling that everything is very simple. We are looking at a real and brilliant and logical world through strange glass.'

Secondly, there is Garner's assured, poetic command of English. The writing in the early books is more fleshy, more prolix than the pared-down economy of Garner's later style, but in books so crowded with incident the restraint of the later Garner would be out of place.

Thirdly, the contrast and juxtaposition of Cadellin and Grimnir reveals an awareness of ambiguity, of life as something more than a simple fight between good and evil. When we first realise that Grimnir speaks with Cadellin's voice and has Cadellin's face we may even think that he is, in some mysterious way, Cadellin; when he is unmasked in chapter 21 he has come 'From the top of Shuttlingslow',[2] where we last saw Cadellin. In fact they are brothers: each has pursued a different path in the way of the sorcerer. The implications of such a close identification of the best and worst characters in the book add a considerable sophistication to what at first sight seems a simplistic moral scheme.

Lastly, Garner commands our belief in his fantasy by rooting it painstakingly and convincingly in a real topography, the Cheshire countryside in which he was born, brought up and still lives.

In an article written in 1968 Garner explained why he wrote about magic and the supernatural impinging on the real world rather than writing self-contained fantasies of the Tolkien type: 'If we are in Eldorado, and we find a mandrake, then OK, so it's a mandrake: in Eldorado anything goes. But, by force of imagination, compel the reader to believe that there is a mandrake in a garden in Mayfield Road, Ulverston, Lancs, then when you pull up that mandrake it is really going to scream; and possibly the reader will too.' The physical backgrounds of all Garner's books are important elements in the stories, be it Manchester and suburban Alderley in *Elidor*, Llanymawddwy in *The Owl Service*, Rudheath, Mow Cop, Crewe and Barthomley in *Red Shift*, or Alderley Edge in *The Weirdstone of Brisingamen, The Moon of Gomrath* and the *Stone Book* quartet (in which Chorley is simply an old name for Alderley). In 'Aspects of a Still Life' Garner writes of his childhood experience of the Edge that 'on that hill, the universe opened'; the process of argument from the particular to the general, from the thing intensely known to the thing intensely felt, lends his early fantasies an inner strength which sharply distinguishes them from the outwardly similar productions of lesser talents.

Alderley Edge and its neighbourhood and the wider

Cheshire landscape have formed the background for all of Garner's work except *The Owl Service*, and has been another connecting, unifying link between the books. Eric Robinson and Geoffrey Summerfield write of John Clare that 'his whole experience centred on the years of his childhood and early manhood in the little village of Helpstone. Thus the whole of his spiritual life is in a sense confined to within a day's walking distance radiating from Helpstone.' The same is true of Garner and Alderley.

In a lecture given to the Folklore Society's Manchester group in 1977, 'Family Oral Tradition and Applied Archaeology in East Cheshire', Garner wrote that 'Alderley Edge is as full of significance and function as is a modern cathedral'. The best section of *The Weirdstone* takes place beneath the Edge; by the time of *Potter Thompson* and *The Stone Book* 'inside the hill' has come to mean 'inside the head'.

The Edge and the life around it has remained the central focus of Garner's work. For an artist enduring the cultural migraine of twentieth-century life to have the stability, the coherence, of a geographically and culturally rooted world-view is clearly a tremendous advantage; assuming, that is, that the artist does not turn his back on the wider world, but rather explores it through the medium of, in David Jones' phrase, the 'actually loved and known'. Garner's continued exploration of his home and background is neither parochial nor inward-looking. It is the fruit of a tension between two cultures, two languages, and a continuing need to balance the damage which being educated into the majority culture did to his sense of himself, as a member of a minority culture, against its intellectual gains. The use and misuse of education is one of his books' chief preoccupations. Their concern with the 'matter of Britain' can be seen as an attempt to relearn and revalue the specifically British modes of thought which have been usurped by the Mediterranean bias of a classical education.

Garner's attitude to the Cheshire landscape is in one sense that of a highly educated linguist and historian, an academic interest in place names and written and oral local history, but in another it is primitive and magical, recalling nothing so much as the attitude of Australian aboriginal tribes to their land. According to Mircea Eliade (whose writings on the history of religions have profoundly influenced Garner's work), 'even the most dreary landscape is, for the aborigines, charged with awe: every rock, spring, and water hole represents a concrete trace of a sacred drama carried out in the mythical times'.

The academic research powers the numinous charge. The sense of a numinous, sacred potency in landscape, in the processes of geology and land formation, pervades the books. It is this rather than any excess of descriptive prose which marks Garner as in his early work a writer about place and in his later a writer about the interaction of place and personality.

Sodger's Hump is remarked in *The Weirdstone* because 'It had the tumulus's air of mystery; it was subtly different from the surrounding country; it *knew* more than the fields in which it had its roots'. The very names of the Cheshire countryside exert an almost hypnotic fascination on Garner, who lists them in *The Moon of Gomrath* as though they form part of a spell or charm:

'Wood and valley and stream swept by, field and hedge and lane, by Capesthorne and Whisterfield, three miles and more, Windyharbour, Withington, Wellbrough';

'They went by Adder's Moss, past Withenlee and Harehill, to Tytherington, and into the hills above Swanscoe, up and down across ridges that swelled like waves: by Kerridge and Lamaload, Nab End and Oldgate Nick, and down Hoo Moor above the Dale of Goyt.'

So in *The Stone Book* when Mary sits astride the weathercock

27

she sees (with one addition from the text Garner reads on record)

> 'all of Chorley, the railway and the new houses. She could have seen home but the Wood Hill swelled and folded into Glaze Hill between. She could see the cottage at the edge of Lifeless Moss, and the green of the Moss, and as she spun she could see Lord Stanley's, and Stockport and Wales, and Beeston and Delamere, High Billinge and all to the hills and Manchester.'

The Cheshire landscape is not a dreary one (as Gowther tells Colin and Susan, 'Folks think as how Cheshire's flat as a poncake, and so it is for the most part, but not wheer we live'): Alderley Edge has retained, despite its use as a popular tourist haunt, a stark, compelling beauty which invites the mind to magic. It is not the particular landscape, though, but the attitude which is important, an attitude which borders on the animistic.

The five chapters of *The Weirdstone of Brisingamen* set in the old mine-workings beneath Alderley Edge (also the setting for part of *The Stone Book*) form the most sustained passage of good writing in the book. The derangement of the senses consequent upon being underground and in the dark is skilfully conveyed, and the atmosphere of lurking terror and alternate claustrophobia and agoraphobia convincingly caught. There are some weak moments (notably the stiff analysis of Colin's feelings about Susan's unwonted courage: she faced danger 'with a composure that claimed his respect even while it nettled his pride'; or the comic-book quality of the later ' "Eeee-agh-hooo!" roared the svarts'), but the drama is inherent in the situation rather than in extravagant incident, and the children's dialogue becomes more and more clipped and realistic. Some of the images are startling in their aptness and originality (the shaft 'ribbed and gleaming like a gigantic windpipe' in the light of Susan's torch; the cave 'into which

28

they fitted like the segments of an orange'), and there are one or two passages of condensed feeling and action which might have been written at any stage of Garner's career. Colin recrossing the plank over the abyss is one such moment: 'Colin willed himself forward. His ears sang, his legs were rubber, his breath hissed through his teeth, his heart pounded, there was rock beneath him.'

Colin rescuing Susan from the plank is curiously like Gwyn calming Alison in chapter 11 of *The Owl Service*. Indeed, one of the reasons why the underground section of *The Weirdstone* is superior to much else in the book is that the children, at least while they are on their own, seem several years older than they do on the earth's surface. Their speech is more lifelike and less bland, and their emotions are subtler. Only in this quasi-adolescent phase of their portrayal do they seem at all rounded or convincing.

The battle between Fenodyree, Durathror and the svarts in chapter 12 is the one lengthy underground episode which rings false. The exchanges between the combatants are contrived and overemphatic, and the actual fighting mere hollow dramatics. This is one of the passages in which the coincidental resemblance to Tolkien, a sharing of sources rather than a direct influence, is too close for comfort. *The Weirdstone* suffers from the artificial, formal, hieratic language into which the narration lapses here, at Cadellin's appearance ('here lay a knight comelier than all his fellows') and at similar points throughout the book. This language, similar to the high 'epic' style affected by Tolkien at crucial points of *The Lord of the Rings,* tends to sound either ponderous or precious. Such passages become fewer as the book progresses, and are noticeably rarer in *The Moon of Gomrath* and entirely absent from *Elidor*. The most damaging instance of such writing in Garner's work is not in his books but in his lush and superficial Christmas story 'The Star of Galgoid' (aka 'Galgoid the Hewer').

The language of *The Weirdstone of Brisingamen* has neither the rhythmic assurance nor the compression nor the directness of Garner's later work. He had not yet found his voice; nor had he won through to a balanced relationship with dialect. In the *Stone Book* quartet the Cheshire cadences and phraseology gradually pervade the narration as well as the dialogue; in *The Weirdstone,* Gowther Mossock (the name is that of the rector of Alderley Church from 1542–1580) bears the whole weight of Garner's wish to employ dialect, which is in essence a desire to recover the speech of childhood. Gowther's speech is not successful: the phonetic spelling, coupled with Gowther's linguistic isolation from the patterns of the narrative, leaves him constantly in danger of collapsing into a sort of received standard yokel: 'By gow, lad, theer's summat rum afoot toneet!'

Gowther can be seen, however, as a flexing of the muscles in the direction of a specifically Cheshire prose, even if he himself seems largely an artistic failure. Some of his phrases recur in the *Stone Book* quartet: 'Now here's wheer we come to a bit of steep', for instance, becomes Robert's 'You'll find you go down a bit of steep' in *The Stone Book.*

Criticism of these two aspects of the book's language, both of which are attempted elevations, and the general comment that Garner is less economical and less precise here than in his best work, should not obscure the fact that in some passages of *The Weirdstone,* usually involving descriptions of the Edge or its atmosphere, he writes with great sensitivity. For instance, when Colin and Susan are trapped in the stone circle (which is not, incidentally, a genuine megalithic monument; it was made by Robert Garner, the stonemason of *The Stone Book,* at the request of Lord Stanley): 'as they faltered, the jaws of the trap closed about them; for, like a myriad snakes, the grass within the circle, alive with the magic of the place, writhed about their feet, shackling them in a net of blade and root, tight as a vice'. Although this sentence is longer than

30

those of his later prose, the word myriad is foreign to his mature vocabulary, the parenthesis 'alive with the magic of the place' is redundant and the phrase 'the jaws of the trap' clichéd, it offers nevertheless a precise and satisfying image, and one which contributes much to the supernatural charge which the very mention of the Edge comes to carry. Roland's terror when trapped inside the stone circle in *Elidor* chapter 3 is, it is true, more keenly felt and vividly communicated than is Colin and Susan's here, but the passage is tightly written, and the episode which follows it, the appearance of Grimnir and his acquiral of the weirdstone, is one of the most successful in the book. The description of Grimnir's 'terrible thinness and spider strength', with 'skin mittens' on 'wasted hands' is remarkably sharp and distinct, and the children's attempt at defiance, their paralysis and his seizure of the stone are related without hyperbole or false drama.

As always in the strong passages of the book (and in his later writing) Garner eschews simile for metaphor: 'his knees were water'. On either side of this passage of strong, direct statement are weaker similes, the grass 'like a myriad snakes', the children's heads pounding 'like trip-hammers'. The moment at which the concentrated intensity of the incident passes can be marked by the reappearance of simile: in one sentence we are simply told of the children's 'wooden bodies'; in the next, they are not dolls but 'doll-like'.

Grimnir's introduction as a chill and a smell in the farmyard in chapter 5 is similarly effective, and contrasts sharply with the weakness of Cadellin's first appearance. The moment at which Cadellin frees the children and scatters the svarts is powerful enough, but the curiously arch idiom in which he speaks deflates him. He never becomes a real character, but remains a stereotype, whereas Fenodyree and Durathror in *The Weirdstone* and Albanac and Uthecar in *The Moon of Gomrath*, for all that they are drawn with crude strokes, share in the plot's vitality. Grimnir's silence is considerably more potent than Cadellin's wordiness.

Sometimes the impact of original or penetrating phrasing is weakened by the surrounding writing: the marvellous expression of distaste for the buildings around Lindow, 'the brick-pocked landscape', is, for instance, enervated by the lecturing tone of the earlier 'The common was encircled by a broken rash of houses, such as may be seen, like a ring of pink scum, on the outskirts of most of our towns and villages today'. Garner's individuality as a writer, however, is not confined to his vocabulary or phraseology, and the first tentative appearance of many of his distinctive traits can be traced in this early work. The use of multiple colons, for instance, which is developed to extremes in *Red Shift*, can be seen in embryo here: 'Llyn-dhu, Lindow: it could be: it *had* to be!'; or, in *The Moon of Gomrath*, 'Believe that help will come: search: try: think of Susan: never lose heart.'

Garner was already aware, too, that some things are better left unsaid. When Colin and Susan venture into Selina Place's magical chamber, around which an atmosphere of palpable evil has been cunningly and skilfully fabricated, the reader is told just enough of what they see to spark the imagination, and not enough to damp it down: 'The pillar was alive. It climbed from out the circle that Selina Place had so laboriously made, a column of oily smoke; and in the smoke strange shapes moved. Their forms were indistinct, but the children could see enough to wish themselves elsewhere.' The fear which the reader's imagination summons is soon given solid form in the hounds of the Morrigan, white with red ears like the dogs of Annwm, with their horrible eyeless snouts and snuffing noses.

The dogs may be akin to the hounds of Annwm, and their owner a Celtic goddess of war, but Garner is concerned as always to link the supernatural with the natural, to use magic to explore life rather than to escape it. The wonders are given precise physical locations; the Morrigan's morthbrood is allied with the creatures of magic but composed of ordinary people, local businessmen and farmers. As Gowther Mossock exclaims, 'You mean to tell me it's the likes of them we've got to run from? I was thinking more of broomsticks and tall hats.' Admittedly, credulity is stretched to the limit when it begins to seem as if Gowther and Bess are the only local people not involved with the witches, and Garner's supernatural net is cast ever wider to include not only svarts, wizards, dwarfs, elves and witches, but the pinheaded trolls the 'mara' (the source of our 'nightmare'), the mysterious Celtic rider Gaberlunzie (the Scottish word for a strolling beggar), prophecy-singing stromkarls and Angharad Goldenhand and her floating island. It cannot be denied that, as the *Glasgow Herald*'s reviewer noted, 'Mr Garner's horrors make Cheshire rather an untidy place'.

The most disturbing aspect of Garner's use of magic in both *The Weirdstone of Brisingamen* and *The Moon of Gomrath* is the seemingly haphazard way in which he incorporates in the books elements of various mythologies. Admittedly, in these books he is not concerned with retelling or reinterpreting tales but simply in using traditional props in an original story, but there is, especially in *The Weirdstone of Brisingamen*, a disconcerting randomness about the introduction of the supernatural. There is little attempt to give 'the world of magic that lies as near and unknown to us as the back of a shadow' a coherent form; the emphasis is on adventure, not metaphysics.

In the afternote to *The Moon of Gomrath* Garner tells us that all the spells[3] and names in it are genuine, because 'a made-up name feels wrong', and that he tries to use names which are 'authentic, yet free from other associations'. In this he often succeeds: Cadellin Silverbrow, Angharad Goldenhand, Celemon daughter of Cei (Cei being Kay, always Arthur's most important knight in Welsh Arthurian tales) and Uthecar Hornskin (an Irish name, unlike the others which are all from *The Mabinogion*) are good examples. Some of the names he uses, however, do have other associations, which do not always tally with the roles accorded the characters using them in Garner's stories. One of the most sympathetic and lively characters in *The Weirdstone of Brisingamen*, for instance, is the dwarf Fenodyree, who is undoubtedly on the side of good, yet the Fenodyree in Manx folklore is a goblin or brownie of hideous aspect and uncertain moral temper. The evil witch the Morrigan is the most powerful aspect of the Irish triple war goddess Badb, who did indeed possess shape-shifting abilities and commonly assumed the shape of a raven or crow. However, Morrigu, although a war goddess, was not an embodiment of evil. K. M. Briggs writes: 'It was Morrigu who infused supernatural strength into Cuchulain, so that he won the war for the Tuatha de Danaan, the forces of goodness and light, and conquered the dark Formorians.'

Morrigu was not always on the same side as Cuchulain, and it was his quarrel with her which led to his death. It is presumably from this that the character of the Morrigan (described by Garner in interviews as based on the mother of one of his old girlfriends) was developed, as Durathror's death scene is copied from that of Cuchulain.[4] This correspondence may have been suggested in its turn by the imagery of the verse retelling of the legend of the wizard, 'The Iron Gates: A Legend of Alderley', printed by Egerton Leigh, in which it was prophesied that when the sleepers awake and drive out England's foes:

> '*Their dabbled wings shall ravens toss*
> *Croaking o'er bloodstained* Headless Cross'.

The headless cross and its attendant ravens is an importation into the wizard of Alderley legend of one of the prophecies of the famous Cheshire prophet Robert Nixon.[5] A compilation of some of the most evocative of Nixon's lines is sung to the children, Durathror and Fenodyree in *The Weirdstone of*

Brisingamen chapter 15, and may well have suggested a number of the plot details they so poetically foretell. Nixon, who is variously dated to the reigns of Edward IV and James I, is, incidentally, the original of the 'Starved Fool' whose prophecies are fulfilled in *Elidor*. Those prophecies seem to be Garner's own, but the story of the idiot ploughboy who spoke true in his fits, was summoned to court, went lamenting that he would be starved to death, and was so in a kitchen cupboard, is Nixon's.

Most of the mythic associations of *The Weirdstone of Brisingamen* are Scandinavian: the svart-alfar, creatures similar to Tolkien's orcs, MacDonald's goblins and the knockers of Cornish folklore, are addressed as the 'maggot-breed of Ymir', the primeval giant from whose body the world was formed in Norse mythology; Nastrond, the spirit of darkness, dwells in Ragnarok, which means literally 'the destruction of the powers', the equivalent of Armageddon; the ravening wolf Managarm that Nastrond sends after those who have betrayed him is presumably to be equated with the Norse Garm, the hound of the underworld; the Fimbulvetir, the 'mighty winter' which is to precede Ragnarok becomes the fimbulwinter, simply another weapon in the hands of evil; Durathror is 'prince of the huldrafolk',[6] the race sprung from those children who were consigned forever to the shadows by a primeval mother ashamed of her prodigal fertility, and swears, among numerous impressive oaths, by the 'Breath of Nidhug', the serpent who lives at the roots of the world tree Yggdrasil.[7]

Grimnir, the symbol of 'the dark powers of the mind', takes his two names from two different mythologies: Grimnir (literally 'the hooded one') is the name taken by Odin in disguise in the Edda; Govannon, as Cadellin addresses him at the end, was the Welsh smith, Govannon ap Don. Govannon was not generally regarded as evil, although he did kill Dylan Eil Ton (the twin of Lleu Llaw Gyffes) for reasons which are obscure. Bearing in mind Garner's conception of Cadellin and Grimnir not simply as brothers but almost as the good and evil aspects of one mind, it seems likely that when he calls Grimnir Govannon he wishes us to equate the wizard Cadellin with the enchanter Gwydion (Huw of *The Owl Service*), in a reference to W. J. Gruffyd's theory[8] that the names Govannon and Gwydion were both derived from the same source (Irish Goibniu/Gavidin). Gruffyd calls such characters 'doublets'.

Grimnir seems to inherit some of his characteristics, such as his foul smell, his aversion to fresh water and his general wickedness from the Scottish monster, the Nuckalevee; he is also half identified with Grendel in *Beowulf*, just as the title *The Weirdstone of Brisingamen* reminds us not only of Brisingamen, the great necklace of Freya in Norse mythology, but also of the Brosingamene, the treasure mentioned in *Beowulf*.[9]

The Moon of Gomrath reveals a radical shift from Norse to Celtic mythology as source material, with much of the symbolism derived from Robert Graves' *The White Goddess*. The moon, as the title suggests, is the central symbol, and it is made clear that Susan, Angharad Goldenhand and the Morrigan represent the three aspects of the moon goddess. All three wear similar bracelets. Susan's is referred to as 'the Mark of Fohla'; Fohla was an aspect of the triple goddess of Ireland (Eire, Fohla, Banbha), and married MacCecht, one of the three grandsons of the Dagda. Susan's magic is of the young, Angharad's of the full and the Morrigan's of the waning moon. The Morrigan's alias, Selina Place, connects her with the Greek moon goddess, Selene.

The story of *The Moon of Gomrath* falls neatly into two parts: in the first, Susan is taken over by a brollachan, the shapeless, speechless evil of Highland legend; in the second Colin is imprisoned by the vengeful Morrigan. In both cases, release is secured by moon magic, and by the use of the Mark of Fohla.

The Moon of Gomrath opens, like its predecessor, with the two children trying and failing to enter the world of magic. The ridiculous shouts of 'Abracadabra' and 'Open Sesame' in *The Weirdstone of Brisingamen* are partly a joke, but the search in *The Moon of Gomrath* is not. Like Mr Noy in the English folktale 'The Fairy Dwelling on Selena Moor' and many other one-time visitors to fairyland, they find that ordinary life has lost its savour after a taste of magic: 'they found it unbearable that the woods for them should be empty of anything but loveliness.'

The magic with which they eventually do become involved has a distinctly different flavour to that of the previous book, and involves a distinction between two sorts of magical power. Cadellin wields the High Magic, which is remote, intellectual, male; to combat the Old Evil of the Brollachan, the children wake the Old Magic, which is intuitive, wild, female, 'magic of the heart, not of the head'. The Old Magic is best represented by the Wild Hunt, which the children unwittingly summon by lighting a fire of rowan twigs and pine ('wendfire') on top of an ancient beacon on the Eve of Gomrath. Gomrath is identified with one of the four great feasts of the Celtic year, presumably, as the book opens at 'the beginning of winter', Samhain, the feast of All Hallows. *Potter Thompson*, in which Garner further explored the legend of the sleeping king, is set on the August festival of Lughnasa.

Garner calls the Wild Hunt the Herlathing, but ignores the figure and story of King Herla, preferring to ally the Hunt with the worship of a horned god, Garanhir, which he translates as 'the stalking person'.[10] He identifies the Hunt with the Einheriar, the bodyguard of the Norse gods, which is, I suppose, fair when one considers how frequently Odin rides at the Hunt's head in English tradition. The first three horsemen to appear, 'the Horsemen of Donn', are the 'three Reds', horsemen of the Sidhe, encountered by Conaire before his death;[11] much of the imagery and language of this whole

37

episode is derived from this story, *The Destruction of Da Derga's Hostel.*

The Old Magic is also moon magic, which is why Colin must wait for the full moon to illumine the magic flower 'mothan' on the old straight track (not the twisting elf road of *The Weirdstone of Brisingamen* but Alfred Watkins' prehistoric ley-line; an alleged straight pathway between sacred sites). The mothan, pearl-wort (Pinguicula Vulgaris), otherwise known as butterwort or bog-violet, was much venerated in Scotland; according to Alexander Carmichael it was 'one of the most prized plants in the occult science of the people'. Carmichael prints several hymns to it in *Carmina Gadelica* (from which, incidentally, the impressive conjuration by which Albanac attempts to subdue the Brollachan in chapter 6 is taken; it is given as 'Exorcism of the Eye').

It is with the help of the mothan that Susan is recalled from 'the Threshold of the Summer Stars' with Celemon daughter of Cei and the daughters of the moon. The Land of the Summer Stars is a name for the Welsh land of the dead,[12] Annwm or Caer Sidi, as is Caer Rigor, which was the riders' stated destination. Cadellin quotes two lines of the *Preiddeu Annwm*:

> *'Three times the fulness of Prydwen we went into it:*
> *Except seven, none returned from Caer Rigor.'*

Prydwen was Arthur's ship. Caer Sidi contains the cauldron of Cerridwen, the Goddess of inspiration, whom Graves identifies with the White Goddess, or the moon. By a process of obscure argument he places Caer Sidi 'at the back of the North Wind',[13] beyond the Corona Borealis, and this seems to be the source of Garner's imagery here. Both times Celemon and her companions appear they resemble Islamic drawings of constellations.[14]

Before the placing of the Mark of Fohla on her wrist sends Susan to join Celemon she is pushed into 'the darkness and unformed life that is called Abred'. This concept of the world as consisting of three levels, and the name Abred, is derived from the mystical writings of Edward Williams, called Iolo Morganwg, the eighteenth-century Glamorgan bard whose faked Welsh manuscripts (which may possibly be based on genuine tradition) deceived scholars for over a century. The concept of the three circles of existence is basic to Iolo's system of bardic/druidic lore (which Garner may have come across in Rolleston's *Myths and Legends of the Celtic Race*). Number 12 of Iolo's 'Triads of Bardism' reads:

> 'There are three Circles of Existence: the circle of Ceugant, where there is nothing but God, of living or dead, and none but God can traverse it; the Circle of Abred, where all things are by nature derived from death, and man has traversed it; and the Circle of Gwynvyd, where all things spring from life, and man shall traverse it in heaven.'

Although Rev. John Williams ab Ithel, who edited many of Iolo's manuscripts posthumously as *Barddas*, notes that Iolo translated 'Cylch yr Abred' as 'the circle of inchoation', it can be seen that Garner's conception of the three circles does not wholly correspond with Iolo's; he has taken what he wants, not what he has found. To Edward Williams, Abred was the circle 'in which are all corporal and dead existences'. Men transcend Abred and attain the second circle, Gwynvyd, by good behaviour. In *The Moon of Gomrath* men inhabit the second circle in this life.

Almost all the names and references in the book are Celtic. The dwarf Pelis the False swears 'by the beard of the Dagda'; Albanac (J. F. Campbell: 'the word Albanach, now used for Scotchman, means Wanderer') is one of the 'Children of Danu', the Tuatha de Danaan, and hears the howls of Ossar, the hound of Conaire that howled three times before he was murdered in Da Derga's Hostel; Angharad gives Susan Anghalac, Finn's horn (not, in tradition, a hunting horn, as

39

here, but a drinking horn);[15] the evil animals employed by the Morrigan are palug and bodach, creatures of Celtic nightmare.

Most of Uthecar's conversation is adapted from J. F. Campbell's *Popular Tales of the West Highlands* (particularly from the first story, 'The Young King of Easaidh Ruadh'), as is some of the Morrigan's (for instance 'Our teeth have long rusted seeking your flesh'). Not only phraseology and cadence are indebted to Campbell; so, too, is incident. The episode with Atlendor, Uthecar and the palug in chapter 11, for instance, is modified from Campbell's story of 'How the last wolf was killed in Sutherland'. The character of the lios-alfar ('they are merciless without kindliness, and there are things incomprehensible about them') owes much to that of the Turks in Campbell's 'The Story of Conall Gulban'. Garner's later *The Lad of the Gad* is an attempt to communicate directly to his readership the emotional charge in the extraordinary stories collected by Campbell, rather than filter it through stories of his own.

Campbell is the primary source; Carmichael's *Carmina Gadelica* is another important one, providing, for instance, Uthecar's redirection of the Morrigan's curse from himself onto the Goldenstone. The original context of these words, phrases and incidents, beyond their Celtic nature and magical significance, is of little importance to their function in Garner's book. They serve, like the names and the spells, to give authenticity to feeling and mood rather than any specific purpose. Only the substantial passages quoted from 'The Destruction of Da Derga's Hostel' in chapter 9 serve a more serious purpose, foreboding doom and destruction.

Albanac, whose end it is that is foreshadowed by the riders, takes on some Arthurian characteristics: the words used of his death or disappearance, in the context of a promise of return, are those which Malory uses of Arthur, 'in thys worlde he chaunged hys lyff'.

40

Although the two early books form a whole, the language of *The Moon of Gomrath* is more controlled and the symbolism more coherent than that of *The Weirdstone*; there is, however, some loss of dramatic impetus. The two halves of the book do not entirely marry, partly because the book was written in two distinct sections. In his essay 'Who, How, Why' Garner writes that 'In Chapter 10 there is a year's gap between the end of the paragraph, "... His eyes were on her, yet she could not be afraid." and the next words, "He stood alone and still in the cold flames." ' It shows.

If the two stories are not bound by any inevitability of movement they are, nevertheless, clearly part of the same book, and that book is not *The Weirdstone of Brisingamen*. The children take on more responsibility, and Gowther and Cadellin, their protectors in the previous book, recede into the background. Gowther does not appear, and is barely mentioned, after chapter 8; Cadellin does not accompany Colin's liberators. Fenodyree is never even mentioned, and his successors, Albanac, Uthecar and Atlendor, are much more inclined to defer to or consult the children.

The Moon of Gomrath is a denser, more poetic book, its images more firmly tied to its theme than was the case with *The Weirdstone*. In places Garner begins to communicate at a deeper level than the adventure story, and to hone his language accordingly. The simple sentence 'Alarm slid across Atlendor's poise like the blink of an eyelid' has no equivalent in the earlier book; likewise, the statement before Susan's climactic confrontation with the Morrigan that 'the air was sweet with fear' is more accurate and less paraphrasable than any similar statement in *The Weirdstone*.

The main criticisms to be voiced against these early books are self-evident. Firstly, Colin and Susan are little more than ciphers. The flatness of the child characters, Garner tells us in 'Coming to Terms', was the result of a deliberate artistic policy: 'The children are my own mistake, but it was done

41

deliberately. I wanted them to be camera lenses through which we look and do not become involved because I wanted to look at the external primary colours of the fantasy.' By the end of *The Moon of Gomrath* Garner was aware of the failure of this idea; his growing dissatisfaction with his bland creations is illustrated by his first ending for that book, in which the Morrigan approaches Colin '& wrung the little bugger's neck'.[16]

Featureless child protagonists were common in children's fiction in 1960, and Garner's are perhaps livelier than many. Certainly his children's lack of character does his fantasy less integral harm than does his lack of control over his material. The books suffer from a surfeit of the supernatural which is only made acceptable by Garner's skill in giving it a local habitation. Garner's later style is distinguished by economy and understatement, but the first two books exhibit the opposite of these virtues: a crude vitality and an emphasis on incident.

Crude it may be, but this vitality should not be discounted. The passage from chapter 8 of *The Moon of Gomrath* in which Colin gives himself totally to his search for the mothan

('On, on, on, on, faster, faster the track drew him, flowed through him, filled his lungs and his heart and his mind with fire, sparked from his eyes, streamed from his hair, and the bells and the music and the voices were all of him, and the Old Magic sang to him from the depths of the earth and the caverns of the night-blue sky')

is a good example of the relentless drive of the text. It shows, too, the unevenness of touch which Garner sometimes evidences in these early books. While the first half of the sentence both forwards the narrative and contributes to and refines the imagery of fire, blood and physical presence which is everywhere associated with the Old Magic (and manages to do so without attributing to Colin any feelings not familiar to every runner),[17] the second half dissipates the tension, relying on stock images, the 'depths of the earth', the 'caverns' of the sky, which, while they do not jar, are of no particular relevance here.

The differences in style and quality between the two books are not great. The surer grasp of source material and more sophisticated and coherent ideas about magic in *The Moon of Gomrath* are matched by the greater energy and more unified plot of *The Weirdstone of Brisingamen*. The magic of *The Moon of Gomrath* is more chilling, more mysterious than that of the previous book, relying as it does on seemingly blind forces of nature, such as the moon, rather than on the kindliness and wisdom of Cadellin. There are some masterful and poetic touches in both books; these may be original, such as the conception of the house where Colin is imprisoned being visible only when the moon shines, or borrowed, such as the moment when Colin catches hold of Susan's hand and 'though it looked like a hand it felt like a hoof', a memory of the Brollachan's last shape as a pony. This is taken from the legend, given in Wirt Sikes' *British Goblins*, of Cadwaladr's goat, which, transformed into a woman, attacks him: 'As for the hand, though it looked so fair, it felt just like a hoof'.

Garner's progress as a writer in the years between *The Weirdstone of Brisingamen* and *The Moon of Gomrath* is best seen not by comparing those two books but by a comparison of the 1960 and 1963 editions of *The Weirdstone*. Even a cursory examination reveals the excision of a host of extraneous clauses, needless adjectives and flabby phrases. The text of the English hardback edition of *The Weirdstone* has never been revised; the 1963 revision which appeared in Puffin was reprinted as an Armada Lion paperback in 1971. The present American hardback edition also gives the 1960 text. Both texts are therefore readily available for comparison, and I will not weary the reader with a long list of cuts. To illustrate my point, the four pages of chapter 1 in 1960 compared with 1963 reveal the following excisions (omitted words in italics): p. 19: '. . . walled gardens of the *big* houses . . .'; p. 20: 'Bess Mossock (*short and plump, with appled cheeks and a smile as broad as her husband's*) before her marriage . . .'; '. . . the heavy meal, *good though it was,* on top'; '*Colin and Susan rolled into bed, blew out their candles, and were asleep almost before their heads touched the pillows,*'; there is also one alteration, of the word 'large' to 'big' on p. 18. The second text is taut where the first one is slack, precise where the first is woolly.

Both books display a number of virtues, a feeling for landscape, a feeling for words and a feeling for story (though not for plot), which won them deserved praise when they were published, and deserved popularity since, but they are by no means representative of Garner at his best. The flaws in plot structure, in the treatment of the characters and in the over-reliance on the materials of folklore are too serious, and too natural to the genre of 'magic fiction', for a rapidly maturing talent to continue in the same vein; although Garner paved the way at the end of *The Moon of Gomrath* for a third book about Colin and Susan he wisely left it unwritten, only returning to the sleeping king legend in 1971, in the much more satisfying form of his libretto for *Potter Thompson*.

2

Garner's third book, *Elidor*, is a bridge between his early and
mature styles, and represents his first attempt to correct the
imbalance he now perceives in his early writing 'between my
ability to express feelings for people and my ability to express
feelings for landscape'.¹ This breakthrough in characterisation is largely confined to Roland, the central figure: the other
three children are never sharply differentiated and the parents
are stock figures, though their monotonous lifestyle is
dissected with gloating accuracy. The most significant
improvement is not in individual characterisation but in the
treatment of relationships: the tension between Roland and
the other children is the first evidence in Garner's work of the
understanding of group dynamics which lies at the heart of
The Owl Service's success.

Elidor² is a separate but parallel world, different to this one
but not wholly self-contained. It is blighted and dying, the
archetype of the wasteland, ruled by a maimed king,
Malebron, who summons four children from our world to his
to save it. The parallel with Narnia, which many readers will
immediately make, reveals the originality of Garner's use of
this conventional device, which he uses to explore the whole
concept of boundaries, physical, mental and spiritual, rather
than to provide a satisfying daydream. Garner has been
criticised for creating a new world and then abandoning it

45

(only five of the twenty chapters are set in Elidor), but he is essentially interested in Elidor as an idea rather than as a reality. Elidor's value is as a point of reference by which we may understand the emptiness and futility of our own world. Our early glimpses of a conventional wasteland (and its parallel in the slum clearance area of Thursday Street)[3] serve to give potency to Garner's notion of suburban middle-class existence as a spiritual wasteland dominated by the television, which is significantly disrupted by the transformed Treasures the children fetch from Elidor, whose power in this world is expressed not in terms of magic but of physics.

Elidor, like all fairylands, is in some respects the land of the dead; more truly, it is the land of spiritual death. The children are taken in turn to the heart of darkness in the Mound of Vandwy in an attempt to regain the three Treasures that have already been captured by the forces of evil. Writing about visits to Caer Sidi, which is called Caer Vandwy in *Preiddeu Annwm*, Robert Graves tells us in *The White Goddess* that:

'The castle that they entered – revolving, remote, royal, gloomy, lofty, cold, the abode of the Perfect Ones, with four corners, entered by a dark door on the shelving side of a hill – was the castle of death or the Tomb, the Dark Tower to which Childe Roland came in the ballad.'

The 'dying of the light' which Malebron regrets is the death against which Dylan Thomas (whose 'Return Journey' Garner had earlier adapted and produced for the amateur theatre) urges us to 'rage'. Before entering the mound Roland has a premonition of death ('he tasted clay in his mouth'); he is actually entering a tomb, New Grange tumulus in Ireland; the hypnotic trance occasioned by the silver apple branch is a type of death; when Roland brings the treasures home 'there was a tension in the silence, as if a clock had stopped'. This recalls the statement in one of Garner's prime sources of background material, Alwyn and Brinley Rees' *Celtic Heritage*, that 'The stopping of a clock in a house which death has visited indicates the supervention of a world where time does not exist'. This idea recurs throughout Garner's work, from the moment in *The Weirdstone of Brisingamen* when 'Reality, space, and time dissolved in the blank, soaring, motionless world' to Joseph's feeling in his excitement in *Granny Reardun* that 'There was no time'.

It may be that the book's ambivalent ending can be explained by seeing Elidor as the land of death, or as a dead land, and regarding Roland's wish to assist Malebron in revivifying it as contrary to nature. To give life to Elidor something else must die, and that something, Findhorn, is almost Roland himself. Garner's unperformed 1971 dance drama *The Green Mist*, based on the fenland folktale retold in *The Hamish Hamilton Book of Goblins*, takes as its theme the necessity of death.

It is the climax of *Elidor* which presents the reader with the most problems. As in all Garner's books the ending is a highly charged, condensed, poetic drawing together of threads; unlike his other endings, that of *Elidor*, while it is powerful, is never wholly clear. It is ambiguous, and seems to elicit widely differing reactions from different readers. What one expects at the end of *Elidor* is for Findhorn (Celtic *fionn*, white = white horn; I suspect the name was taken from section V of David Jones' *Anathémata*, '*this* is the sound of the Findhorn stone!') to become a self-sacrificing messianic figure, dying to give life. This is not what happens, and we are left with the feeling that Findhorn is an unwilling sacrifice, and that Elidor is not made worthy by his death, but cheap. There is, mixed with relief that the children are safe and that Elidor will be restored, a strong sense of loss, of anti-climax, of wrongness. After the 'glories' of the fusion of the treasures in the 'golden light':

'The song faded.
The children were alone with the broken windows of a slum.'

47

The last sentences are downbeat and depressed, and Findhorn an uneasy figure.

Interviewed by Justin Wintle in 1974 Garner claimed that the book was 'nihilistic' (a word he has since repudiated to me), and that 'if the book had gone on for another page Roland would have gone mad'. This was the first public expression of his view of *Elidor* as a Platonic fable, in which 'At the end you realise that Elidor is just another parallel and not a superior world; and the cost of achieving Elidor is the death of reality'. In 1979 when I asked him to expand on this he said:

'The whole of the background philosophy, physics and metaphysics of *Elidor* is closely connected with Platonic philosophy, and very simply what is revealed throughout the book and made clear at the end to the children is that of the children who are protagonists the one who appears to be the materialistic lout, that's the eldest, Nicholas, is in fact the most sensitive. He has intuitively picked up from the start that there is something very wrong going on, and this appeared quite fortuitously in the book, because I thought that he was a materialistic lout, but when there is the breakthrough by the people of Elidor, when they actually manifest themselves in the garden, and just run across the garden and jump over the fence, I was shocked by what Nicholas did, because I didn't plan it. He picks up stones and throws them after them wildly, in a totally psychotic way, and he's crying. Now that is something I didn't plan at all, I wasn't even aware it was coming. It was so startling I wondered if I should just cut it immediately, but I left it in; it was right. Now, Nicholas has seen that it is *wrong* to meddle. The fault of Roland is that he's always had dreams of an ideal state and he makes the mistake of assuming that Elidor, and all that has to do with Elidor, Malebron, is this perfection that he's always felt, in his dreams, and so he devotes himself to furthering that end, in fact he's driving himself in an egocentric way to produce a power within himself that he's not felt before, and that is not shown by his brothers and sister. Nicholas intuitively works against this, and at the end, and it's very clear to children, when Roland looks into the eyes of the dying unicorn he sees the Platonic archetypal reality and realises that in order to secure Elidor, which he thought was reality but was only a parallel strand of Plato's shadows at the back of the cave, it was only another shadow, he has sacrificed reality, that the cost of the simulacrum was the reality, and that's why he was going mad.'[4]

For Garner, the significance of the book seems to be that Roland discovers at the end that, as in chapter 3, 'What he had imagined to be the music of his dreams was only the jingle of a half-learned tune'. Roland deludes himself into thinking that Elidor is the country behind the wall in H. G. Wells' story 'The Door in the Wall',[5] a land of 'immortal realities'; by their actions he and Malebron, seeking to restore Elidor to splendour, invoke, summon an elemental, Findhorn, 'all fire and air', into both worlds, and destroy him.

I do not find this explanation (which is not, it should be made clear, an account of Garner's motives in writing *Elidor*, but of the patterns he saw in it subsequently) entirely convincing, though it sheds some light on the book's main area of mystery. To perceive in *Elidor* a structure parallel to that of *The Owl Service,* with a similar reversal of sympathy between the male leads at the end, the unsympathetic Nicholas usurping Roland in the role of hero just as Roger replaces Gwyn, is a possible view of the book, but not one to which I can subscribe. Roland does gain our sympathy early on, and never loses it, though he may at times seem pig-headed; Nicholas never really gains it, though he may at times seem sensible.

It seems to me that the ending of *Elidor* only makes sense if it is viewed as a mixture of bitterness and exultation: Roland 'cried his pain', but also 'for an instant the glories of stone, sword, spear and cauldron hung in their true shapes, almost a trick of the splintering glass, the golden light'. If Garner wanted the reader to feel that 'The cost of achieving Elidor is the death of reality' then with me, at least, he has not succeeded. It seems to me to end, like *The Moon of Gomrath*, in 'joy and anguish'.[6]

We are left with a number of difficult elements, one of which is the character of Malebron, in which there is a sinister undercurrent with which critics of *Elidor* have never really come to terms. Children's book convention insists that a guide such as Malebron be an unequivocally good figure, but Malebron's name warns us that this will not be so.[7] He is in some senses egotistical, unyielding, almost psychotic. His sentences, liberally scattered with exclamation marks, are almost always commands. Nicholas' speech in chapter 11 is crucial:

> 'It's all mud and dust and rock. It's dead, finished. Malebron said so. And you should think about him a bit more, too. Did he care how we made out as long as he found his Treasures? He sent us trotting off into that Mound one after the other, but he didn't go in himself. What right has he to expect us to spend the rest of our lives like – like broody hens?'

It was the meeting between Malebron and Roland in chapter 4 which caused Garner most difficulty, and he was still rewriting it five months after finishing the rest of the book. In the radio play from which it sprang and in the early versions of the novel, Malebron is polite and reassuring, and often calls Roland by name. A visit in August 1964 to the Chichester production of Peter Shaffer's *The Royal Hunt of the Sun*, with Robert Stephens as Atahuallpa, showed him where the error lay: 'I had to take the warmth out of the meeting and put in manipulation and fear.'[8] These qualities, as Garner pointed out to me, are later emphasised by echoes in Malebron's exhortations to the children as they flee Elidor ('Think!

50

Move!') of Pozzo's curt orders to Lucky in *Waiting for Godot*. Garner had in fact already sketched this mutually ruthless relationship in 1961 in a deleted passage from *The Moon of Gomrath*. On Angharad Goldenhand's island Susan muses:

> 'Angharad's using me for her own reasons, she thought. I suppose it's right about Selina Place; the cats would have got me, and I shouldn't know about Colin; but she's done it all to wreck Selina Place – not to save me. All right: but she's not going to get rid of me when it's over. If I've got this power, I'll know a lot more before this is finished, and then we'll see how Cadellin'll shut us out of Fundindelve.'

The only trace of this spirit to survive in the book is Susan's manipulation of Atlendor at the close of chapter 15, but it is clearly the source of Garner's later conception of the relationship between Roland and Malebron, which he had sketched out on his return from Chichester (see plan on following page).

Shaffer's play (whose slangy conquistadores may have contributed to the coarse colloquialisms of Garner's Roman soldiers in *Red Shift*) is, like *Elidor*, much concerned with death. At the centre of the play is an ambiguous, fraught relationship between the representatives of two cultures, Atahuallpa king of the Incas and Pizarro his conqueror, who seem at times identified with each other, at times mirror images of each other, and at times father and son, son and father. *The Royal Hunt of the Sun* must have made it clear to Garner that the radio Malebron's courtesy and concern were an impossibility: that he was driven by pride, and the reckless assumption of his own importance. Shaffer's stage direction describing Atahuallpa's movements may serve to isolate the element of Atahuallpa's character which determined Malebron's development: 'When he moves or speaks it is always with the consciousness of his divine origin, his sacred function and his absolute power'.

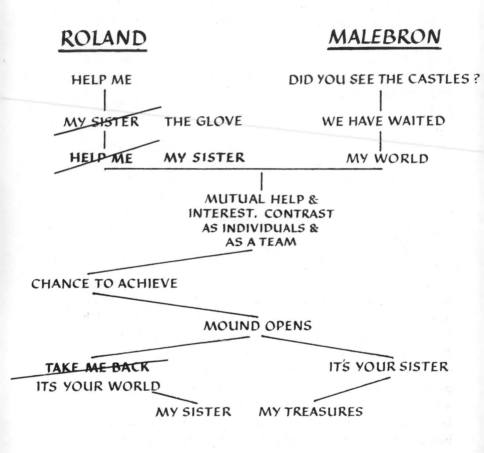

Malebron, whom Garner associates privately with Epstein's famous statue of St Michael at Coventry Cathedral,[9] is also, as Carolyn Gillies perceptively noted in her article 'Possession and Structure in the Novels of Alan Garner', to some extent Roland's twin or alter ego, and is this book's expression of Garner's most abiding theme of deep psychological ties between individuals. Cadellin and Grimnir in *The Weirdstone of Brisingamen*, Susan, Angharad and the Morrigan in *The Moon of Gomrath*, Gwyn, Roger and Alison and their historical and mythical counterparts in *The Owl Service*, Tom, Thomas and Macey in *Red Shift*, the four children in the *Stone Book* quartet and Roland and Malebron in *Elidor* are all explorations of the same mystery, of which Garner's story 'Feel Free' is his most single-minded account. Roland also, in his incoherent glimpses of Elidor in chapter 1, allies himself with the visionaries with whom Garner becomes increasingly concerned from this point in his career. His staccato speech could belong to Huw, Thomas or Macey: 'See? I didn't – see. I – through my fingers – See? Towers – like flame. – A candle in darkness. – A black wind.'

Elidor's most important stylistic advance on the first two books is in the amount and the quality of the dialogue; it is an advance traceable directly to the interviewing work which Garner was doing for Granada Television in the early sixties. Not only did the experience of recording, listening to and editing street interviews teach Garner how to listen to what people really said, it also taught him how to present it. In an article on *The Owl Service* printed in the Manchester Grammar School Magazine *Ulula* in 1968, Garner wrote, of being a writer in the latter half of the twentieth century:

> 'Not least of the gains for the writer is a technological one: the portable tape recorder. For the first time it has become possible to examine the structure of unguarded speech. Dialogue can now be used so accurately that a single line may replace a page of narrative prose. This is

53

not to say that such dialogue is easily written. The difference between good and bad is the difference between an edited BBC interview and Uncle Fred's tape of last year's Christmas party.'

That Garner's work for Granada and for BBC radio had a direct influence on *Elidor* can perhaps most clearly be shown by reading the following transcript, of a recording of boys aged about 12 in the slum clearance areas of Manchester and Salford, made just prior to the writing of the book, with *Elidor* chapters 6 and 7 in mind:

> 'When they're dropping a house, we hide, and then run into the middle while the dust is clearing, and they think they've killed somebody when they see us standing there. They're dead scared, and sometimes they give us half a dollar to tell nobody, but usually they shout at us, and we laugh and run away.'

Elidor started life as a half-hour radio play, which ended when the children returned to Manchester with the grail talismans. The text of the play, which was written at great speed to meet a deadline, is close to that of the book's early chapters, and this may account for the feeling that, as in *The Moon of Gomrath*, the book is in two parts which do not entirely marry.

It must be said, however, that the qualities of *Elidor* are such as to make it rewarding as well as puzzling reading and that it represents a great advance on the first two books. Garner is no longer capable of writing, or rather leaving unaltered, a sentence such as the final one of part 1 of *The Weirdstone of Brisingamen*: 'And it was as though a veil had been drawn across the children's eyes.' His writing has bite and tension. Partly the tension derives from the isolation of Roland from his siblings (even on the first page he is 'a few yards away' from the others; the physical distance indicates the psychological and emotional ones), but mostly it is brought about by the exceptionally clear, concise, economical style. Garner is moving towards shorter sentences, fewer adjectives, less explanation; towards a style like the quartz in which Roland finds Helen's glove: 'white: cold: hard: clean.'

The precision and concision of the writing ('the cold thrill and burn of the spray' that Roland feels in chapter 2; the history of Elidor and its troubles related in ten lines in chapter 4), which anticipates the clipped, expressive sentences of *Red Shift*, is only one of the qualities which are emphasised by a comparison of *Elidor* with André Norton's *Steel Magic* (1965; London, 1967), a book which offers many analogies. In *Steel Magic* two brothers and a sister enter Avalon through one of its four gates and are met by Huon of the Horn, who tells them that they have been summoned to save Avalon from the encroaching dark: 'by spells and treachery three talismans have been lost to us: Excalibur, Merlin's ring and the horn'. Just as in *Elidor*, 'When we drive back the dark and hold it firmly in check, then peace reigns in your world. But let the dark surge forward here, winning victories, then in turn you know troubles, wars, evil.' How much more effective is Malebron's quiet understatement: 'the death of Elidor would not be without its echo in your world'.

Because *Steel Magic* is set almost wholly in Avalon there is no need for a careful balancing of the two worlds, or for these mutterings about the relationship between them to be made explicit in action. Huon tells the children that 'Only in Caer Siddi, the Castle Foursquare, may we learn the truth'; they go there, and then set out in search of the treasures, armed, whimsically, with a stainless steel knife, fork and spoon which assume gigantic proportions. Although *Steel Magic* is, as are all Norton's books, competently written, there is a lack of power in the talisman/symbols which prevents the quests from seeming urgent. The children's acts of bravery and daring are overly melodramatic, and their characters flat, while the action is hampered by stilted dialogue. Seeing the

55

same themes (there is in *Steel Magic* as well as *Elidor* a brother, Eric, who does not trust the fantasy world and tries not to succumb to it) handled by another author highlights Garner's virtues, particularly his command of dialogue and his ability to avoid the fey and whimsical. The realism of *Elidor*'s setting shades fantasy into metaphysics; the fake medievalism of *Steel Magic* pushes it into superficiality.

The four Treasures which Garner's children rescue, a spear, a cauldron, a sword and a stone, may be identified with the four Treasures of the Tuatha de Danaan (the spear of Lug from Finias, the sword of Nuada from Gorias, the cauldron of the Dagda from Murias and the stone of Fal from Falias),[10] with the four main symbols of the Grail legend, with the tricks in the Tarot pack, the four Hindu castes,[11] the contents of the Ark of the Covenant, the flesh-hook, cauldron, shield and sword given by Maedoc to Bandubh King of Leinster,[12] with their counterparts in the list of the 'Thirteen Treasures of the Isle of Britain',[13] and presumably a number of other things too. The symbolism is widespread. The physical appearance of the cauldron links it with Cerridwen's cauldron as described in the *Preiddeu Annwm* 'with a ridge round its edge and pearls'.[14]

Roland has the spear, Helen the cauldron, David the sword, Nicholas the stone of kingship. It is only the first two, however, which actively contribute to the symbolism, and indeed after chapter 6 the Grail symbolism becomes diffuse and weak. In many ways the Treasures' function is no more clearly defined than that of the weirdstone in the first book, and their effects are described in similar terms. Cadellin tells Colin and Susan that 'while there is light in Fundindelve, the sleepers lie here in safety'. Malebron's first, urgent question of Roland is, 'Is there light in Gorias?' The Grail imagery in *Elidor* is also an extension of the pictures conjured up in Colin's and Susan's minds by the howl of Ossar in *The Moon of Gomrath* when the land itself is seen as a type of the Grail, full of 'hollows filled with water and fading light'. As Helen carries the cauldron 'light splashed and ran through her fingers like water'.

The Grail symbolism is never coherent, and its sexual resonances never explored: Findhorn the unicorn tends to supplant Roland in the latter half of the book. The incest between Child Roland and 'his sister proud Eline' in the Danish ballads of Rosmer Hafmand in Jamieson's *Popular Ballads* and *Illustrations of Northern Antiquities* is not possible or desirable in *Elidor*, but it is this unstated theme which gives Findhorn's death its emotional charge. Helen's 'I've broken it' implies both a loss of virginity and, in reference to her clumsy breakage of the unicorn jug in chapter 11, an acceptance of responsibility (which Roland cannot give).

Garner does make oblique use of the continuation of the Roland story in the Rosmer Hafmand ballads in his 1980 TV play *To Kill a King*, in which the author hero, perhaps Roland grown up, is confronted by his muse singing the ballad of 'Child Waters'.[15] The Scottish version of this ballad given in Jamieson's *Popular Ballads* is called 'Burd Ellen', and by analogy with the Danish ballads it seems to me, though this is impossible of proof, to represent a sequel or companion piece to the story of Child Roland. After Child Roland's dark tower, in Child Waters' castle 'of redd gold shineth the tower'. It is clear that the main reason for using 'Child Waters' in *To Kill a King* was because it mentions Cheshire, but the parallel with Child Roland seems inescapable.

Roland may be to some extent identified with Findhorn, but there remains a feeling that the replacement of the Grail knight and his spear by the unicorn and his horn left Roland virtually redundant at the climax. It is Findhorn who makes Helen cry, thus 'freeing the waters' of Elidor.[16] His symbolic act of procreation, when he lays his head in the 'makeles mayde' Helen's lap, and his ritual sacrifice replenish Elidor's guttering fertility. Roland's sense of futility and helplessness at the end is, of course, intended, but it is yet another disturbing feature of the book's climax.

Garner may not have intended any Christian symbolism in the figure of Findhorn, but the identification of Helen with Mary (Garner actually uses the medieval 'I syng of a maydn that is makeles' in *Holly from the Bongs*) combined with the theme of sacrifice inevitably introduces Christian connotations. In a way, the unicorn theme is a method of reintroducing Christian thought into the recovered pagan Grail legend of the four Treasures. The unicorn is here, as often, to some extent a Christ figure, and so, too, is Roland,

> *'Her Thursday's child*
> *come far to drink his Thor's Day cup'.*[17]

David Jones' mingling of Christ, Odin and Peredur in this section of *Anathémata* is clearly germane to Garner's intention in *Elidor*.

Findhorn is a standard unicorn of tradition, and his capture deliberately echoes the description given by Gerard Legh in his sixteenth-century heraldry textbook *The Accedens of Armorye*:

> 'When he is hunted, hee is not taken by strengthe, but onelye by thys pollicye. A mayde is sett where he haunteth, and shee openeth her lappe, to whom the Unicorne, as seeking rescue from the force of the hunter, yeldeth hys hed, and leaveth all his fiercenes, and resting himselfe under her proteccion, sleapeth untill he is taken, and slaine.'

Findhorn's song is less explicable, though bearing in mind Findhorn's relationship to Roland it may be relevant that the violinist Neaera in Louis MacNeice's radio play *The Dark Tower* learns Roland's name from a swan: 'He sang your name and he died.' Another reference to which Garner himself drew my attention also encourages the identification of Roland and Findhorn, for the speaker is addressing himself. It is the self-pitying monologue of the comic butt Sir Gefferey Balurdo in Act V of Marston's *Antonio's Revenge*:

'O colde, colde, colde, colde, colde. O poore knight, o poore sir *Gefferey*; sing like an Unicorne before thou dost dip thy horne in the water of death; o cold, o sing, o colde, o poore sir *Gefferey*, sing, sing.'

'Sing: oh, sing' implores Roland. Marston, it should be noted, was a native of Coventry, whose cathedral provided not only, in Epstein's St Michael, one image of Malebron, but also, in the form of Piper's baptistry window,[18] the glorious image of the 'morning' in *Elidor*, when 'a sun-burst swept the land with colour'. This image is a joyous, affirmative one, and is the culmination of the book's Christian undertones. It does not suggest to me that Elidor was not worth saving.

Findhorn's death is echoed in the Bushman folktale 'The Young Man, the Lion, and the Yellow-Flowered Zwart-Storm Tree' which Garner retells in *The Guizer*. At the end of the tale, which Radin characterises in *The World of Primitive Man* as 'the tragedy which inevitably follows when man either overreaches himself or fails to understand his limitations, to understand the fundamental realities nature and the gods impose upon him', the lion which has pursued the young man it has marked out as its own accepts its own death along with his.

'Then the lion spoke at last, saying, "Now I am ready to die. For I have the young man that I put in the yellow-flowered zwart-storm tree, the young man whose tears I licked, the young man that I have all this time been seeking. Now I have hold of him, for I am his." '

The lion is Findhorn, the young man both Roland and Helen. In early drafts of *Elidor* when Helen begins to cry 'The tears dropped on Findhorn's muzzle from her open eyes'.

The story of Child Roland, a folktale which has come down to us in a curious *cante-fable* form, half-prose, half-verse,[19] provides the dynamics of the first half of the story, but no deep or obscure symbolism. Once the apparatus of church, ball, fairyland and rescue by Roland of his sister and two elder brothers has come into play, once the children have reached Elidor and found the Treasures, then the folktale has no further role to fulfil. Roland's adventures in Elidor owe as much to the Grail legends (the standing stones, based on Avebury, represent his ordeal in the Chapel Perilous; Helen's glove embedded in quartz is the black hand which often appears in the Chapel; the castle is the Grail castle from *Sone de Nansay*) as to 'Child Roland', though the Mound itself (a combination of Silbury, New Grange and Maes Howe) accords well with the Dark Tower of the tale, both in atmosphere and detail. The magic branch which has set Helen, Nicholas and David to sleep is a Celtic addition: it was found by Cormac mac Airt in the year AD 248 according to the annals of Tigernach;[20] a similar branch sends Bran, son of Febal, to sleep at the beginning of *The Voyage of Bran*. Similar sleepers, who have 'laid hands on the bell-branch and swayed it, and fed of unhuman sleep', are described in Yeats' 'The Wanderings of Oisin'.

The Grail symbolism, the unicorn and the Child Roland story are supplemented by references to twentieth-century psychical phenomena: the Treasures' effect on household equipment recalls a similar incident at a house in Salisbury in 1920;[21] the planchette writing resembles the Borley wall writings[22] (the planchette unicorns are medieval watermarks from C. M. Briquet's classic *Les Filigranes*);[23] Roland's sensation in chapter 1 that the church is 'flat, like a piece of stage scenery' follows that of the two English women, C. A. E. Moberly and E. F. Jourdain, whose eerie experiences at Versailles at the turn of the century gained wide circulation in their pseudonymously published *An Adventure*.

At the heart of Garner's use of these mythological or supernatural materials in *Elidor* is the concept of myth as the gauge of liminal experience, as the bridge between two states of consciousness. 'Wasteland and boundaries: places that are neither here nor there – these are the gates of Elidor.' As Alwyn and Brinley Rees put it: 'boundaries between territories, like boundaries between years and between seasons, are lines along which the supernatural intrudes through the surface of existence'.

The map the children spin and follow to Thursday Street is to some extent a maze, the ritual traversal of which will lead from one state to another; Garner refers obliquely to such mazes in both *The Stone Book* and *Potter Thompson*. At the start of the book the children are in a state of inactivity, hung between two homes (the door in the wall 'is not found by seeking'; the Reeses write 'in some of the "Voyages" it is when the voyagers have lost their course and stripped oars – when they are not going anywhere – that they arrive in wondrous isles'); Findhorn breaks through in Boundary Lane; the static electricity around the Treasures is most noticeable at dawn and dusk.

The descriptions of Elidor's past greatness are based on the quotations about Tir-nan-Og from *The Voyage of Bran Mac Febail*, *The Voyage of Condla Ruad* and *The Wooing of Etain* given by Alfred Nutt in his introduction to Rev. James MacDougall's *Folk and Hero Tales,* source of several stories in *The Guizer* and the Finn story which Garner contributed to William Mayne's *The Hamish Hamilton Book of Heroes*:

> 'Fair is that land to all eternity beneath its snowfall of blossoms . . . the gleaming walls are bright with many colours, the plains are vocal with joyous cries, mirth and song are at home on the plain, the silver-clouded one. No waiting there for judgement, naught but sweet song to be heard. No pain, no grief, no discord. Such is the land.';

'No death, no sin, no decay, but ever we feast, and need none to serve us, ever we love, and no strife ensues'; 'A magic land, and full of song; primrose is the hue of the hair, snow-white the fair bodies, joy in every eye, the colour of the foxglove in every cheek.'

The children's adventures should probably be seen in the context of Irish *immrama* or voyages such as *The Voyage of Bran, The Voyage of Condla Ruad* or *The Voyage of Maelduin* (which Garner included in *The Hamish Hamilton Book of Goblins*). In *Celtic Heritage* Alwyn and Brinley Rees suggest that the *immrama* were stories 'to teach the craft of dying'; Celtic equivalents of the Tibetan Book of the Dead.

In his lecture, 'Inner Time', Garner wrote that 'Man is an animal that tests boundaries . . . and the nature of myth is to help him understand these boundaries, to cross them and to comprehend the new.' While the nature of the boundaries crossed by the children in *Elidor* is unclear, I suspect that the chief boundary is that of death rather than sexual or social maturity. The story's varied elements never resolve into any clear or coherent statement, and such concerns remain submerged.

Elidor is a book without a still centre, a book which presents different and contradictory aspects at each new reading. Garner's, and our, ambiguous attitude to Malebron, Elidor and the Treasures, and the split between the book's Elidor and Alderley sections, prohibit any assured or dogmatic response. Garner's main achievement in *Elidor* was to refine his use of myth so that its power is concentrated rather than diffused. He was unable, however, to supply a logical connection between myth and reality, as he was to do triumphantly in *The Owl Service*. The only reason we are given in *Elidor* for the children's involvement with the supernatural is that Roland is 'highly strung' and 'always imagining things'. *Elidor* is not, however, simply a string of mythologically based incidents, as its predecessors were.

There is for the first time, despite the triply fragmented setting, a sense of fate unravelling; the events of the narrative form an ordered whole.

In *The Owl Service* and *Red Shift* this sense of structure becomes obsessive: each incident, each phrase is set in careful relation to every other incident, every other phrase in the book. The unity of thought of which this is the most visible symptom derives to a large extent from the quality and quantity of research which goes into each book. In 'A Bit More Practice', written in 1968, Garner explained his writing method, which involves a long period of purely scholarly research followed by a fallow period followed by a creative phase in which the results of the research are synthesised in a fictional context. The list of research topics for *Elidor* seems, as he says, absurd, and is largely an attempt to establish his intellectual bona-fides for the readers of *The Times Literary Supplement*, but it does give some idea of the intensive preparatory work which his method of writing involves:

> '. . . in the third book, *Elidor*, I had to read extensively textbooks on physics, Celtic symbolism, unicorns, medieval watermarks, megalithic archaeology; study the writings of Jung; brush up my Plato; visit Avebury, Silbury and Coventry Cathedral; spend a lot of time with demolition gangs on slum clearance sites; and listen to the whole of Britten's *War Requiem* nearly every day.'

The repeated listenings to Britten's *War Requiem* (which was, of course, written for the re-dedication of Coventry Cathedral), are another indication that *Elidor* is a book about death. But though their themes chime, Britten's work seems to have had little direct influence on Garner's book, barring the occasional verbal echo ('the hopelessness', *Elidor* chapter 3, refers us back to Wilfrid Owen's 'Strange Meeting', one of the poems set by Britten). The wasteland, as often, has some of the characteristics of the First World War trenches.

The *War Requiem* is clearly influential not on *Elidor* but on much of Garner's subsequent writing: for instance, the repeated 'Sleep you on' which closes *Potter Thompson* complements Owen's 'Let us sleep', which concludes Britten's work. The *War Requiem*'s threefold structure (the ritualised response of the mass, the personal one of Owen, and the ethereal boys' choir; past, present and eternity), with final reconciliation of the three elements (chorus and orchestra, soloists and chamber group, boys and organ), may well have influenced the form of both *The Owl Service* and *Red Shift*. Both world wars form a sub-theme in *Red Shift*, and a major one in *Tom Fobble's Day* and *The Aimer Gate*. *The Aimer Gate* at least is clearly indebted to Owen, in feeling if not in detail.

The *Elidor* research list is not simply the result of an author's eagerness to convince us that his books are not just kiddies' stories; it tells us something important about Garner's work. His books are not just the result of inspiration or visionary imagination, though without the inspiration they would be worthless; the research is a way of validating and containing the vision. Garner writes in 'A Bit More Practice' of his work on Welsh history, language and law in preparation for *The Owl Service*: 'Nothing may show in the book, but I feel compelled to know everything before I can move.'

3

The Owl Service, the novel with which Garner won the Carnegie Medal and the Guardian Award, and in which he fulfilled the promise of the earlier books, is the only one of Garner's novels without a Cheshire setting. The action takes place in Llanymawddwy in Wales, which Garner conceived as the setting for the story of Lleu Llaw Gyffes in the Fourth Branch of *The Mabinogion*.

It is a rich and subtle work, interpreting a contemporary story of possessive love, jealousy and class division through the symbolism of the *Mabinogion* story. The two stories are, indeed, inextricable, although Garner has chosen at various times to stress one or the other (in 1976: '*The Owl Service* is an expression of the myth found in the Welsh *Math ap Mathonwy* – and only incidentally concerned with the problems of first-generation educated illegitimate Welsh males'; in 1970: 'When I read the legend, I felt that it was not just a magical tale, but a tragedy of three people who destroy each other, through no fault of their own, but just because they are forced together'). *Math ap Mathonwy* is a simple story of betrayed love: the enchanters Math and Gwydion make Blodeuwedd out of the flowers of the meadowsweet, the oak and the broom as a wife for Gwydion's son Lleu, whose mother Arianrhod has prevented him from ever having a human wife. Blodeuwedd falls in love with Gronw Pebyr and, with pretend concern, discovers from Lleu the conditions under which he can be killed. Gronw fulfils the conditions, but Lleu does not die; he is changed into an eagle (see 'Loki' in *Goblins* and 'Maui-of-a-Thousand-Tricks' in *The Guizer*). Gwydion finds a sow at the foot of a tree eating the decaying flesh which the eagle is dropping, charms Lleu down and restores him to life. Lleu in his turn then kills Gronw; Gwydion turns Blodeuwedd into an owl as a punishment for her crime.

The basic premise of *The Owl Service* is that this ancient tragedy has been periodically re-experienced, as the power unleashed in the valley by the manufacture of a living woman from flowers continues to build up and seek expression, either as flowers, as Blodeuwedd was, or as the flower-faced owl into which Gwydion turned her in his wrath. 'Lleu, Blodeuwedd and Gronw Pebyr. They are the three who suffer every time, for in them the power of this valley is contained, and through them the power is loosed.'[1] As Kathleen Raine writes in 'On the Mythological' in *Defending Ancient Springs*: 'a real event may be the enactment of a myth, and from that take on supernatural meaning and power'.

In a sense *The Owl Service* is another book about the Waste Land. The valley is 'sick', and the three adolescents, Gwyn, Roger and Alison, must face the consequences of their bitter triangular relationship to restore it to health. Release of the power may destroy those involved, but its function in the valley is regenerative. Holding measures employed by previous generations to keep the power at bay, by channelling it into the dinner service of the title, the painting in the billiard-room or Bertram's stuffed owl, have only increased the pressure on this generation. Though both the gossiping women in the village shop and the later taxi-driver and chorus of villagers diffuse rather than intensify the power, at its best the book is suffocatingly claustrophobic and intense. The small cast, the enclosed valley and the oppressive weather make the reader as aware of the discomfort of the characters' enforced intimacy (of them all, Gwyn and Alison are the only ones ever entirely at ease with each other) as the characters themselves.

As often in Garner's writing, children must learn to cope with their parents' failure to confront their problems, and in this case the situation is further complicated by the presence on the scene of the survivors of the last explosion of power: Nancy, Gwyn's bitter, narrow mother, the cook, and Huw Halfbacon, the gardener, who is simple-minded and lucid by turns. Huw (Halfbacon is one of the nicknames of the enchanter Gwydion, Lleu's father, whose descendant Huw, and through Huw Gwyn, is, and whose exploits Huw recounts as his own) is a prophetic fool, and is regarded by the other characters with a proper mixture of contempt and awe: contempt, usually, from the 'educated' English; awe and respect from the Welsh villagers. He looks back to the 'Starved Fool' of *Elidor*, and the earlier reliance on Nixon's prophecies, and forward to the epileptic heroes of *Red Shift*.

Huw, like Gwydion, attempts to help and guide Gwyn; Nancy, like Arianrhod, tries to stymie him. It seems likely that we are meant to regard Huw and Nancy as brother and sister, and Gwyn as an incestuous as well as illegitimate child, like Lleu before him; Garner's suggestion in 'Coming to Terms' that Margaret, Alison's mother, refuses to allow her daughter to see Gwyn because she suspects that the dead Bertram (Gronw to Huw's Lleu and Nancy's Blodeuwedd) fathered both is not inferrable from the text (though it is clear from the book, and more especially from episode 5 of the television serial, that Margaret's interest in Bertram has been more than cousinly), and I suspect that he was gently pulling his audience's leg rather than offering serious exegesis. Class prejudice is a more straightforward motive.

The central question in any consideration of *The Owl Service* must be how well Garner has integrated his mythological and realistic concerns; the most serious criticism of it is that by treating of an adolescent pash he has trivialised his source material.[2] I cannot accept this view: the contemporary story is more tragic, not less, because of the characters' social immaturity. Garner captures precisely the brooding, in-turning intensity of adolescent passion, the peculiar vulnerability of adolescent selfishness; it is important to his theme, of the valley's power using only those minds apt to it, that his characters should inhabit the border country between childhood and adulthood, 'adolescence, (when) the potential universe is open to our comprehension'.[3] In a sense all myths, being the expression of primitive kernels of emotion rather than its sophisticated developments, are adolescent dramas; Lleu, Blodeuwedd and Gronw Pebyr are adolescents in emotion (and in their reliance on Math and Gwydion as father figures) if not in years. The love of the story must be first love or none at all, the hate first hate.

The strong, simple outlines of the adolescents' story form only the third part of a narrative web of great complexity. Like *Red Shift*, *The Owl Service* has three narratives unfolding at the same time, each affecting the other in numerous perceptible and imperceptible ways. The three stories of *The Owl Service*, of Lleu, Blodeuwedd and Gronw, Huw, Nancy and Bertram, and Gwyn, Alison and Roger, unfold simultaneously, with none of *Red Shift's* intercutting, but the basic literary device is the same in both books.

That the contemporary story should be played out against the backdrop of the sour ruins of the previous generation's tragedy, and under that generation's jealously watchful eye, adds an emotional resonance which transforms the story from a simple tale of adolescent passion to a penetrating comment on the human predicament; it adds to the intensity of the myth a social consciousness, in which each character is placed into a complex relation to all the others which takes into account not only the eternal values of myth but also the English class system, the English domination of Welsh culture and the problems of the 'generation gap' (which in Garner's writing is seen as the inevitable result of parents visiting their own failures and inadequacies on their children). In this context the *Mabinogion* story offers the perfect model of human relationships, containing the seeds of any number of different stories.

It is not, however, simply in this sense of a universal model to which the other two stories in *The Owl Service* can be referred that *Math ap Mathonwy* is used. It is, rather, an active force, in what is, as Garner wrote in *Filming The Owl Service*, 'a kind of ghost story'. Garner seems now to regret the eruption of the myth into the tale: in 'Coming to Terms' he says that 'One of the weaknesses of the book is that I brought too much of *The Mabinogion* into it because I could not leave it out'. Aidan Chambers writes in *The Reluctant Reader* that 'the explicit intrusion into the story of the Fourth Branch of the Mabinogion is, to my mind, a weakness in the book, rather than a strength'. However, while I agree that the device by which bits of *The Mabinogion* itself rather than the *Mabinogion* story are incorporated into the text is somewhat clumsy, it seems to me that the supernatural elements in *The Owl Service* serve brilliantly to knit the three strands of the narrative together, and create a powerful and condensed symbolic alternative to the weighty pages of psychological analysis which would otherwise seem necessary to convey such an emotionally tangled situation. Alison's vision of Blodeuwedd in the stone fish tank; Roger's apprehension of Lleu's spear as 'a blink of dark on the leaves'; Gwyn's discovery of Gronw's spear head 'so thin that the moon shone through it, and the fretting of its surface made it a leaf of sculpted light and stone', are key moments, for which satisfactory 'realistic' alternatives would be hard to find. The whole structure of the book is dominated by that of the Fourth Branch: how else can Gwyn be made to confront his fate but by Gareth Pugh's sow? How else could the story's tensions find resolution but by the subtle manipulation of the symbolism of owls and flowers?

To say that the *Mabinogion* story is indispensable to *The Owl Service* is not to suggest that the modern story is a mere mechanical reproduction of the myth.[4] The central relationships are moving and convincing without *The Mabinogion*: the myth gives them their structure, but the tragedy comes from inside the characters, is not imposed upon them. Although *The Owl Service* refers constantly to *The Mabinogion* there is nothing in it which needs to be explained outside the book's own terms of reference. To read *The Owl Service*, then *The Mabinogion* and then *The Owl Service* again is to have one's experience of the book enriched, but not fundamentally changed. Lack of knowledge of Garner's source is no impediment to the enjoyment of the book, and could not be if it is to be considered a success. It may even be detrimental to a first reading to bring too many preoccupations about the Fourth Branch to bear on *The Owl Service*.

This said, the points at which the stories do touch are manifold: meadowsweet, for instance, pervades the whole text, either in perfume or actuality, from the moment Gwyn steps into the attic in chapter 1 to the last page. Such touches, and refinements of them such as the smell of goat which Roger detects on the meadowsweet by the Llech Gronw,[5] and Roger and Clive's appreciation of the spear-hole in the stone as 'a crafty precision job',[6] abound, and are scarcely worth chronicling. The important correspondences are those between the mythological and contemporary characters. The parallels between Gwyn and Lleu are particularly rich. Gwyn, according to Robert Graves, was the 'autumn name' of Lleu when he was a god.[7] Gwyn is killed emotionally by Roger's sneers after Alison has betrayed his vulnerable point; he is prevented from leaving the valley and chased up a tree by a wandering black sow; he is called down from the tree by the singing of Huw/Gwydion. However, like Govannon and Gwydion, Lleu and Gronw are but two aspects of the same character, and it is not necessary for the reader to make a specific connection between Gwyn and Lleu. In 'Coming to Terms', Garner said: 'if you follow the text closely, in fact Gwyn equals Lleu, Gronw equals Roger. If you see it the other way round that is fine, because that is how the myth works.'

As in *Elidor*, the forces of magic and the supernatural are seen as analogous to those of modern physics, particularly electricity, and Garner makes this point through two powerful metaphors which recur throughout the book: the valley is a 'reservoir' of power; the three who enact the drama are the wires by which the power is conducted. Alison is the live wire, and at the critical moment when Gwyn, cold and unforgiving as Lleu Llaw Gyffes, remains neutral, it is stolid, unimaginative Roger who makes the loving commitment necessary to earth the power and turn Blodeuwedd from vicious owls to harmless flowers. The emergence of Roger as the decisive, courageous figure at the end is signalled (his conversation with Huw in chapter 9, in which he remarks that 'That bloke Gronw was the only one with any real guts: at the end', is particularly significant)[8] but it comes as an enormous shock. The reader is encouraged throughout to sympathise with Gwyn, and the strength of the ending is that even though our expectations have been overturned it appears retrospectively to be the inevitable and correct solution. Opinions about the ending of *The Owl Service* differ sharply. To many it seems a betrayal of Gwyn, to be a cheat, executed by sleight of hand; to others, myself included, it seems the high point of the book, the moment at which Garner casts aside the Fourth Branch and sets his characters free. It is the only strong ending possible which would resolve the book's tensions rather than obliterate them: for Gwyn to forgive them would sentimentalise the book, denying the importance of what has gone before; for Roger to be destroyed, like Gronw, would offer the reader no hope. The ending is prepared for, it is organic, and it is the lynchpin of the book.

The image of Alison, Gwyn and Roger as live, neutral and earth was emphasised in the imaginative eight-part television serial of the book, with scripts by Garner himself. Alison dressed mainly in red, Gwyn in black, Roger in green; thus they carried the inevitability of the ending with them from their first appearance. The colour symbolism was extended in numerous ways: the wall in the billiard-room splits, for instance, when three snooker balls of the appropriate colours crash together.[9] Garner had the leisure, in eight episodes, to keep very close to the original text in his dramatisation, and much of its quality transferred to the screen, helped by a camera which continually tightened the screw of tension by seeking the angle which would unnerve as well as portray.

The Owl Service is not a fantasy, but a novel about human relationships, a tripartite examination of the destructive power of possessive love. It is perhaps most clearly distinguished among Garner's works for its taut, uncanny evocation of fear. The ability to communicate fear is one of Garner's finest qualities, and a fairly constant one (for instance the climb through the mine-shaft in *The Weirdstone of Brisingamen* chapter 14, the horror emanating from Mount Vandwy in *Elidor* chapter 6, Mary's vertigo-inducing ascent of the steeple in *The Stone Book*), and it is in *The Owl Service* that he utilises this gift most fully. Gwyn's discovery of the owl-pellet in *The Owl Service* chapter 6, for instance, is chilling, and absolutely necessary to the plot. Garner is never needlessly frightening (though some of the stories he chooses to re-tell, such as 'The Flying Childer' and Campbell's tales in *The Lad of the Gad*, are horrifying): he recognises the purgative value of fear. He admires Japanese legends because 'they have the real touch of fear in them',[10] and writes approvingly of the Celts that 'no other people were so rich and terrifying in their imagination'.[11] When asked to choose his 'favourite' short story for inclusion in the anthology *Author's Choice* he rejected the concept of 'favourite' and chose instead 'the most terrifying story I know'. It should be noted that the story, Marghanita Laski's 'The Tower', has as its central symbol a 'dark tower'.

The most significant artistic advance in *The Owl Service* over Garner's previous writing is in the depth and subtlety of the characterisation. Clive, who is first sketched as 'Jo-jo' in chapter 15 of *Elidor*, is perhaps too given to jovial cliché, Alison too weak, Roger too unimaginative, Gwyn too fiery and tempestuous, but despite these suggestions of exaggeration the characters are both rounded and convincing. Even Alison's mother, who never appears, is a felt presence; her character is built up slowly but in great detail by hints and implication, and the quality of the experience available to a reader of the book is to a certain extent determined by his or her ability to infer, almost from the interstices of dialogue rather than from any direct statement, a fully-fleshed picture of her. This new awareness of the intricacies of character is matched by the perceptive exploration of subtle class distinctions, not only between the 'subjected' Welsh and their English overlords but also between the nouveau riche Clive and the snobbish Margaret; distinctions which operate powerfully at a submerged level among the younger generation.

These distinctions are expressed in the modulations of the language. Garner is very skilful, for instance, at indicating, without saying, when Huw and Gwyn are speaking Welsh and when English. Such episodes as Gwyn addressing Alison with a bitter string of mock-Welsh clichés in English are effective because the reader becomes highly attuned to such nuances. The book's peculiarly Welsh atmosphere is achieved without contrivance: the Welshness lies deep in the cadences of speech, not in snippets of the Welsh language or, except for ironic purposes, smatterings of Welsh cliché.

Ravenna Helson, in her article 'Through the Pages of Children's Books' in *Psychology Today*, made a most perceptive comment about *The Owl Service* which may serve to explain both the hint of exaggeration in the characterisation and the fact that this does not jar on the reader. She wrote: 'The characters represent different forces within the personality, and a compelling sense of the interrelation of these forces permeates the story.' Whether or not this was intended in *The Owl Service*, and I do not imagine that it was, Garner certainly used this technique deliberately in his 1980 television play *To Kill a King*, in which the main action is a surrealistic charade peopled by aspects of the sole 'real' character's mind. The central character, a writer with a block, achieves a release of inspiration when his two externalised aspects, a fussy male secretary and a bitchy sister, have driven him to the point at which he realises that he is trapped by the weight of his past, by his public image, and must destroy it to proceed. The play is the first example (other than the very minor 1962 radio play *Have You Met Our Tame Author?*) of Garner drawing on his adult life for his subject matter, and in this context it is interesting to note that the medal which Harry, the writer, shuts away before he can write, and which may be identified with the stone head he throws into his television set at the play's climax, is Garner's Carnegie Medal, which he won, of course, for *The Owl Service*.

Certainly *The Owl Service* has none of the stock figures and empty ciphers of the early books; instead, we find character delineation of great delicacy and insight, communicated almost entirely through dialogue. This reliance on dialogue, which is an extension of the style which Garner was developing in *Elidor*, coincides with a general pulling in of the slack in the narrative tone. The fleshy 'poetic' padding of the earlier books is shed to lay bare the nerve: 'Her face was bone and thin as a man'. The style is taut, economical, restrained; the emotion leashed in, concentrated. Emotional turmoil is expressed not by hysterical scenes but by analogy with the forces of nature, for instance the violent storm in which the climax is played out. In itself this may not be a very original idea, but it works extraordinarily well in *The Owl Service*, perhaps because the electric storm strengthens and gives body to the insistent use of electricity as a metaphor for mythic power.

At its best this highly condensed style merges myth, history and reality into one, as when Nancy, like Blodeuwedd before her, walks backwards out of the valley, in a string of images of crystal purity: 'She walked backwards up the road, shouting, and the rain washed the air clean of her words and dissolved her haunted face, broke the dark line of her into webs that left no stain.'

4

Halfway through *The Owl Service* Garner wrote a Nativity play, *Holly from the Bongs*, for his local school. It was published, with photographs of the preparations and performance by Roger Hill in 1966, and in 1971, in his note in John Rowe Townsend's *A Sense of Story*, Garner thought it his 'one complete success'. It is indeed a subtle and powerful work, of which the final scenes especially are dramatic poetry of a high order. By drawing parallels between the mystical rebirth ceremony of the traditional mumming play, of which a version is performed by the shepherds, and the Nativity, Garner manages to include in the Nativity story a version of the Passion and the Resurrection, and to encompass the sadness as well as the joy of the festival. The mumming play is a composite version, but it has its own voice; it is far removed from the blandness of the 'normalised' text given in E. K. Chambers' *The English Folk-Play*.

Garner roots the Bible story firmly into a Cheshire background. Joseph and the shepherds speak broad Cheshire, and the end of all is that

> 'Now may you Jesus see
> By Goostrey's heart and boundary.'

It is Goostrey, not Bethlehem, that this Jesus has been born in, and the gifts the modern children bring him, the justification to Mary of her sacrifice, are

> *. . . holly with berries from the Bongs,*
> *And leaf upon linden light from Galey Wood:*
> *Bracken from Bomish, Broadway and Blackden:*
> *Apple and medlar from No Town Farm.'*

Holly from the Bongs was an exciting development in Garner's writing. Aidan Chambers has written, in 'Letter from England: The Play's the Thing' that *'Holly from the Bongs* is a peak in Alan Garner's work. He achieves in it – the only occasion in his prentice work, by which I mean everything up to *The Owl Service* – a balance and harmony of heart, mind, content and technique. *Holly from the Bongs* is a moving and brilliant Nativity play.'

I can but agree. It is a work of great poetic force, and represents Garner's writing at its best. The intense, heightened awareness which grips his characters is revealed with a brilliant simplicity and directness:

> *'I cannot see.*
> *Me eyes are mithered*
> *By that light*
> *Outside. The bright*
> *Flame and wings and the sky*
> *All feathered fire:*
> *And now the fierce cold star*
> *Like a dagger.'*

Like the *Stone Book* quartet *Holly from the Bongs* insists on being approached as a whole, not piecemeal. The blunt dialogue of Joseph and the shepherds, Mary's calm, wise resignation, the liveliness of the shepherds' play and the exuberance and laughter of the modern children combine to form a perfect unity; it deserves to be more widely known. Set to music by Gordon Crosse, who also composed the music for *Potter Thompson,* it was performed in Manchester in 1974, and filmed by the BBC. It is an exceptionally pure example of

77

Garner's ability to articulate the universal by concentrating on the local.

The short, sharp prose of the introductory section of *Holly from the Bongs* is echoed in the picture book *The Old Man of Mow*, also with photographs by Roger Hill, which was published in the same year. In it, two boys search for the Old Man of the title, only to discover at the end that he is the curious rock formation on which they had first seen his name chalked. Written with a hard clarity, the book is a charming if off-beat production, and interesting as yet another example of the hold which the Cheshire landscape exercises over Garner's imagination. It is a straightforward book, and its main claim to our attention is as a more detailed comment on the highly charged setting of *Red Shift*. It provides the interested reader with a guided tour of some of that novel's sacred ground given by the author himself.

It was inevitable that Garner's interest in folktale and in storytelling would spill over into the twilight area of folktale retellings for children, and his first project after *The Owl Service* was *The Hamish Hamilton Book of Goblins*, a contribution to a high-quality series of compilations whose other editors included William Mayne and Roger Lancelyn Green. *Goblins* is an exceptional work in an area noted for mediocrity. The stories have been chosen with care and insight, and retold with sensitivity, and they resonate to *The Owl Service* as *The Guizer* does to *Red Shift*.

In *Goblins*, for instance, Paul's arrogance in 'The Trade that No One Knows' is Gwyn's; so is the prince's ruthlessness at the close of 'Bash Tchelik', which is Garner's addition. We see the *Owl Service* story, too, in the search for the secret of Bash Tchelik's death. Glooskap is compared by Spence, Garner's source, to Lleu Llaw Gyffes, though the basis of the comparison lies outside the portion of Glooskap's story which Garner chooses to retell. The various Welsh pieces are by-products of the *Owl Service* research.

The editing policy varies, and in his afternote Garner distinguishes three levels of treatment: adaptation, free adaptation and transposition. The adapted stories keep close to the source texts: 'Yallery Brown' and 'The Green Mist' from Mrs Balfour's extraordinary 'Legends of the Lincolnshire Cars' are simply shorn of their obscurities of dialect, as is the terrifying 'The Flying Childer' from the same source, which was printed in Leon Garfield's *Baker's Dozen*. The Irish tales, 'The Voyage of Maelduin' and 'The Adventures of Nera', keep close to the translations of Stokes and Meyer; too close, sometimes. In 'The Voyage of Maelduin', for instance, when we hear that Nuca the wizard specified an exact number of men for the crew of Maelduin's boat it seems pointless except in an academic context to retain Stokes' (and the manuscript's) 'seventeen men, or sixty according to others'. Similarly, the sentence, identical in Garner and Stokes, 'When they had gone a little from land, after hoisting the sail, then came into the harbour after them his three fosterbrothers, the three sons of his fosterfather and fostermother; and they shouted to them to come back again to them to the end that they might go with them' seems unnecessarily confused.

In general, though, Garner's treatment of Stokes' text is sensible. "Tis' becomes 'It is', 'thy' becomes 'your', 'marauders' becomes 'raiders', the Christian references are removed, and a number of uninspired or incomplete chapters omitted. Of these only chapter 14, the powerful Miller of Hell section, is to be regretted. As Stokes gives it it is incomplete, and although it is clear from Garner's notebooks that he is familiar with 'The Voyage of the Húi Corra', in which this incident is repeated, an unwillingness to tamper more than necessary seems to have prevented him from filling in one's gaps from the other.

An indication of Garner's scrupulous treatment of sources, and also of his delight in words used precisely but out of their

79

ordinary context, can be seen in his preference for the literal 'bald' in the phrase in chapter 1 'they found two small bald islands' as opposed to the more conventional 'bare' which Stokes supplies, relegating 'bald' to a footnote. Similar reversions to literal meaning rather than the more easily intelligible but more prosaic paraphrase recur in *Goblins* and proliferate in *The Guizer*.

In the lengthy version of 'Ramayana', too, Garner refrains from impressing his own personality on the text, except in so far as selection and inclusion implies a coincidence of theme in source and transmitter. Coomaraswamy's version was one twentieth of the length of the original, and Garner halves it again. His main creative effort seems to have gone into reparagraphing rather than rewording, breaking up the story into acceptable small fragments without interrupting the flow. He does not attempt to alter the stiff, formal, though poetic, style of his source: Sita asks Hanuman 'do you speedily bring Rama here'; Coomaraswamy's 'Thereat the deities rejoiced' is altered only to 'Thereat the gods rejoiced'.

In general Garner scours his tales clean of formal or nineteenth-century phraseology, but 'Ramayana' is from a written source and like 'Sir Halewyn' in *The Guizer* is respected as such. His dealings in 'Gobbleknoll', 'Moowis', 'Great Head and the Ten Brothers', 'The Smoker' and 'Glooskap' with Lewis Spence's unyielding prose are more typical. 'In the long ago there existed a hill of ogre-like propensities' becomes 'There was a hill that ate people'. 'The Smoker' is hardly even a story in Spence. Similarly in 'Vukub-Cakix' only the barest outline is taken from Spence; most of it is as 'original' as any of Garner's work, though it is not, I think, one of the better stories in the book, remaining always somewhat sketchy.

With the Japanese tales, which form the fourth major strand in the book after the Celtic, the English and the American Indian, Garner was able to follow his sources more closely, but he still adds, alters and refines to a considerable extent. Almost all the direct, colloquial dialogue in 'The Goblin Spider', for instance, is Garner's, and several of his additions reflect his own recurrent themes. In Davis, his source, the tale ends 'Raiko heard the welcome sound of a cock crowing and imagined that the ghostly visitors would trouble him no more'; in Garner, Raiko must keep the goblins at bay till dawn because then 'they will have lost a gate into the world'. Davis' 'countless cobwebs' becomes in Garner 'a billowing web of stickiness' which is compared, in a daring and poetic image, to the visitant's hair. The last curt, chilling sentence is also Garner's addition.

Similarly, his style in 'Hoichi the Earless' is punchy and terse; irrelevancies and unnecessary circumstantial detail are ruthlessly excised. When the priest sees Hoichi without his ears in Lafcadio Hearn's version, part of his speech runs 'I trusted my acolyte to do that part of the work; and it was very, very wrong of me not to have made sure that he had done it! . . . Well, the matter cannot now be helped; we can only try to heal your hurts as soon as possible . . . Cheer up, friend! – the danger is now well over. You will never again be troubled by those visitors.' All this becomes in Goblins the simple, laconic, ' "It is difficult to write on ears," said the priests.'

The Hamish Hamilton Book of Goblins is a testament to the extent to which Garner has remained faithful to the first tales which caught his imagination in the twelve Harrap volumes belonging to his great-grandfather he describes in his after-note to the book. The vast majority of the stories in Goblins can be found in the relevant Harrap volume, as can most of Garner's mythological interests, if only in embryo. Rolleston's Myths and Legends of the Celtic Race, for instance, includes the story of Lleu Llaw Gyffes, the story of Da Derga's Hostel, a section on Iolo's 'Circles of Being', Stokes' 'Voyage of Maelduin', Preiddeu Annwm, the four treasures of the Tuatha de Danaan, and so on.

81

Much of *Goblins* is also pre-echoes of *The Guizer*: the first story, 'Gobbleknoll', is clearly part of a Hare cycle; John Connu in Andrew Salkey's poem is the animal-masked trickster of *The Guizer* part 1; Loki is pure guizer. The two Loki stories, 'Loki' and 'Baldur the Bright' are interesting in that they derive from two of the three radio plays based on Norse mythology which Garner wrote in 1965 and revised in 1978. Except in plot they bear little resemblance to their source, Brodeur's translation of the prose Edda; they have been completely recast. The vivid, lively dialogue gives these stories a special vitality, and they are the most successful stories in the book. The plays, particularly in their second incarnation, are also excellent.

The plays are very close to the stories, but there is a general sharpening of tone and diction in the 1978 versions. In these, too, the Norse gods are revealed as Cheshire gods: when Loki spots a hut in 'Thor and the Giants' Thor's reaction marks him a Houghite: 'It'll do, whatever it is. Better than sleeping outside, anyroad, Loki. Mm. It's summat and nowt: more like a tent: rum tent, though.'

Only occasionally do the plays expand the stories, perhaps most effectively in the narrator's description of Hel's home: 'The name of her hall was Misery. Her plate was Hunger. Her knife was Greed. Idleness was her manservant, Sloth her maid; Ruin her threshold; Sorrow her bed; and Conflagration her curtains.'

The Norse stories are not the only part of *Goblins* to draw on Garner's radio work: 'The Secret Commonwealth' and 'Wild Worms and Swooning Shadows' are closely based on the first two programmes in his 1963 quartet on British folklore 'Merlin's Isle'; some of the other stories ('Yallery Brown', for instance) were used in the remaining programmes.

The Hamish Hamilton Book of Goblins also saw the first appearance of a motif which was to recur later in Garner's writing: the three heads in the well. The extract from Peele's *Old Wives' Tale* in *Goblins* is also sung by the Boy in *Potter Thompson*, and the story to which it refers is the strongest of Alan Garner's *Fairytales of Gold, The Three Golden Heads of the Well*.

This story is essentially 'The Wal at the World's End' from Chambers' *Popular Rhymes of Scotland*, the tale Englished by Norah and William Montgomerie as the title story of their *The Well of the World's End*, improved by sensitive additions from other British versions of the tale. Jacobs' 'The Well at the World's End' provides the sieve, the opening and the 'Stop it with moss' rhyme; Halliwell's 'The Three Heads of the Well', the heads' other songs and the incident of the queen's daughter hitting the heads with her bottle; Cheshire speech provides the evocative 'yellow-bellied askers' which the queen's daughter emits. The introduction of the water's changes of colour (by analogy with tales such as the Grimms' 'The Fisherman and his Wife') is a stroke of genius in a picture book text, giving Michael Foreman, the illustrator, a chance to excel.

The other changes are equally beneficial: 'ye nasty dirty beasts' becomes 'You round bobbing beast'; 'she'll be ten times bonnier' becomes 'she'll be bonnier yet'. Only the translation of 'Weird, brother, weird, what'll ye weird?' to 'Say, brother, say, what do you say?', inevitable to retain the sense, is to be regretted.

Garner's approach to 'The Wal at the Warld's End', editing and amending with reference to other versions, is repeated in the other three *Fairytales of Gold*. He almost seems to have deliberately chosen stories which were in need of repair: the two stories elided in *The Girl of the Golden Gate*, 'The Girl Who Went Through Fire, Water and the Golden Gate' and 'The Glass Ball', both from Addy's *Household Tales*, are two of the weakest in the whole corpus of English traditional tales. Unfortunately the combination does not secure their strengths but rather exhibits their weaknesses. *The Girl of the Golden*

83

Gate shows an uncharacteristic lapse of judgement in the retention of the girl's 'Oh, you don't know how glad I am' when she finds the golden ball, an exclamation which only makes sense if, as in the source story, she has been lured into the fox's service in search of the lost ball. The insipid ending (not much stronger than the trite conclusions of Addy's tales) is interesting only for its echoes of the scene in *The Moon of Gomrath* when Susan enters the spinning wheel of her bracelet and steps onto Angharad Goldenhand's island.

The Golden Brothers is a vivid retelling of one of the most widespread of all folktales 'The Twins or Blood-Brothers', of which the only version in Katherine Briggs' *Dictionary of British Folk-tales*, 'The Fish of Gold', is a damaged example, featuring only one golden son, one golden lily and one golden foal. Garner restores the duality, which is the basis of the story's appeal (and is also, as is the good and bad daughter theme in *The Three Golden Heads of the Well*, a direct treatment of one of Garner's major preoccupations) and adds some details from elsewhere. The bearskin which the first brother wears as a disguise, for instance, can be found in the Grimms' 'The Golden Children'. Many versions of this tale[1] include a dramatic dragon-slaying episode, which Garner ignores. As it is, his story lacks tension. Usually the second brother would sleep with the first brother's wife, a two-edged sword between them. Without this, the ending seems peremptory and abrupt.

The Princess and the Golden Mane combines two tale types, 'The Louse-Skin' and 'The Youth Transformed to a Horse'. It is the most original of the four, and it proceeds with a startling, dream-like lucidity and a meticulous inner logic. The ogre's gruesome refrain of 'More to a meal than ears and thumbs' is appropriately chilling. The basis of the story is a Persian tale, 'The Magic Horse', given in M-L. von Franz's *Shadow and Evil in Fairytales*, but the ogre's phrase, with all its subterranean potency, came, Garner tells me, in a dream.

It is perhaps significant that Garner only started to approach folktale and myth directly in *The Hamish Hamilton Book of Goblins* after he had finished *The Owl Service* and discarded myth as an overt presence in his fiction. From now on retelling and writing were to move in tandem rather than together.

5

Alan Garner was already talking quite fully about his next novel *Red Shift*, then calling it *Not Really Now Not Any More*, in 1967,[1] but the prediction of one of the journalists to whom he spoke that 'As profound research will not be necessary it should not take years to write' proved somewhat optimistic. The book took six years to complete, and is the apotheosis of Garner's allusive, elliptical, condensed style. It is a novel about time in the same sense that *Elidor* is a novel about space.

Of all Garner's books *Red Shift* elicits the strongest reactions: Bob Dixon condemns it for its 'general atmosphere of hopelessness and degeneration'; Elizabeth Cook, in similar vein, objects that 'the young people have become brutalised and the language bludgeoning'; Marion Zimmer Bradley observes that 'The meaning of the title is just as obscure as everything else about this book, and the most interesting character in it was the Stone Age hand-axe'; Konstantin Bazarov wrote in his review that it was 'a bad attack of gimmicky self-indulgence brought on by overpraise', and announced that 'It was a relief to turn from this to *The Stainless Steel Rat Saves the World*'. Conversely, Edward Blishen praised 'the almost vicious forward movement', and Aidan Chambers 'the terrible accuracy of the dialogue'. The confusion and the controversy seem to stem from the fact, noted by the anonymous *TLS* reviewer, that 'It is probably the most difficult book ever to be published on a children's list'.[2]

To some the book is incomprehensible, incoherent and pretentious; to others it seems overwrought, hysterical, or simply too distressing.[3] Its perceived faults, however, often seem to lie more in the assumptions of its critics than in its text.

One of these assumptions, which still applies in the world of children's books, is that reading is a passive activity, and that narrative connections should be explicit, rather than implicit. Garner was not interested in writing a traditional 'beginning-middle-end' narrative; he was not even primarily interested in establishing a forward flow. His interest lay rather in 'the effort to commemorate, to mark the flux'; to balance 'momentum' with 'memento'.[4] The story of *Red Shift* is the story of the reader's creative response to the text: the surface appeal which keeps us turning the pages is essentially the need to forge links between the three narratives rather than to find out what happens next in any one of them, though that desire, too, plays its part.

Time in *Red Shift* is perceived not as a continuum but as continuously present, and the three stories develop, both independently and interdependently, with no sense of one being contemporary and the others 'history', until in the last few pages they fuse into a single undifferentiated time. Many critics seem to feel that the two chronologically earlier stories, set in the early second century AD and December 1643, are subordinated to the contemporary story, and some even view them as distractions from it. This seems to me to be the result of the reader's search for a book which fulfils a set, expected narrative pattern rather than a flaw in *Red Shift*, in which the weight of the narrative rests fairly equally on all three strands. Another school of thought[5] holds that the resolution of Macey and Thomas' visions into Tom's 'blue and silver train' trivialises the earlier stories, particularly that of the

Barthomley massacre, which is an historical incident. However, Garner's interest in the Barthomley massacre is not in the organised violence of the massacre but in the individual violence in the web of relationships between Thomas, Margery, John Fowler and Thomas Venables; similarly, he dwells not on the My Lai-style massacre carried out in Barthomley by his fugitives from the shattered Ninth Legion but on the individual tensions inside the group and on the violent treatment of one individual, the unnamed girl. The book's basic premise is that the most important, and the most difficult, task in life is the establishment of loving contact between two people, the breaking down of barriers, and it is against this private, internal struggle that the seemingly random violence of the outside world is measured, rather than vice versa. In his 1972 'One Pair of Eyes' television film . . . *All Systems Go . . .*, which exhibited many of the faults *Red Shift*'s critics claimed to find in the book and included an embarrassingly overplayed, improvised dramatisation of *Red Shift*'s opening scene, Garner wrote, 'Our emotions are as violent as the stars, and won't be denied, no matter how hard we try'. That he intends Tom's domestic trauma to equal in pain and horror the more dramatic massacres of the earlier incidents is clear from Tom's choice of reading matter in the more economical and effective film Garner later made of the book: Aeschylus' *Choephori (The Libation-Bearers)*, in which a son kills his mother at the command of a god. Just as Orestes performs his matricide off-stage, so Garner dispenses with the physical act and relates only the mental violence.

I will inevitably have to deal with the three narrative strands separately to some extent, but our understanding of each rests heavily on our reading of the others: they are, in fact, inseparable, locked in a delicate and subtle balance. The parallels between the stories go much deeper than a simple sharing of geographical setting and the axe talisman: every sentence is a comment not only on the immediate action but also on the rest of the book. Ideas, words and phrases are reworked compulsively until they acquire a mantra-like resonance, and the simple final statement (whose real meaning is, of course, the opposite of its surface one) that 'It doesn't matter. Not really now, not any more.' can stand for the whole.

This graffito, which Tom and Jan find in the ruins of Thomas and Margery's house on Mow Cop (and which Garner saw on the walls of a station waiting room, adding resonance both to the choice of Crewe station as meeting ground and to Tom's dismissal of Jan's home: 'It's only a waiting room now') haunts the book, rising to the surface of the text at significant points: when Macey starts to come to terms with his profaning of the sacred axe; when Tom reveals that he has done so by selling it; when Thomas tells John he no longer wishes to smash it; momentarily when Macey buries it.

Each of the stories centres round a love relationship, although the contemporary one is a more introverted, claustrophobic affair than the others. The three men are linked by their possession of the axe, by their vulnerability to fits, by their sense of mental dissociation from themselves, and by their name (Macey is a diminutive of Thomas), which means 'twin', and is also a common name for a fool. Macey is vaguely aware of Thomas and Tom, feels Tom's hands pressing on his eyes and sees Barthomley Church and the tower on Mow Cop, although they are not yet built, and Thomas sees Tom's face and hears 'echoes backwards' in his fits; Tom seems unaware of the others, but obscurely troubled by the weight of past sadnesses. Often experiences reverberate, like the words of the graffito, through all three stories: Margery wraps the thunderstone[6] in her petticoat dyed with alder (her 'red shift'), and the narrative cuts to the girl asking Macey 'When did the god come to you' as she paints him with alder; Jan drawing a stone across her hand recalls the hamstringing of the Barthomley girl; both Thomas and Tom read out the words 'Let there be no strife, for we be brethren' from the church screen at Barthomley, and both Margery and Jan reply 'How do I know?', while 'Let there be no strife: for we are brothers' are some of Macey's 'big words'.[7]

In all three cases it is the women who understand and manipulate the gift of the axe-head: it is 'the moon's axe',[8] and once again the moon and instinctive magic are identified with the female principle. It is the captured tribal girl, the embodiment of the corn goddess, who recognises that Macey is intermittently possessed by a god; it is Margery who restrains Thomas from smashing the thunderstone; when Tom sells the axe, and explains that it was 'votive', Jan's shocked rebuke is that 'You had to be told that': she has always known that it is sacred, a 'Bunty'. The specific indentification of the 'Cat' girl with the corn goddess can be extended to the other two: they are further representations of the White Goddess, the instinctive female who is at once terrifying and alluring, confusing and comforting. So, too, is Tom's mother. Not until *The Stone Book* does Garner produce a female character who is not primarily a passive vehicle of natural forces, a creature of instinct, acted upon rather than acting. Alison in *The Owl Service* is incapable of willed action, unable to make any choice between owls and flowers or between Gwyn and her mother. This view of women hinders *Red Shift* as much as it helps it, and it is an element of Garner's work which I will consider at greater length in chapter 8.

It may be that some readers feel the lack in *Red Shift* of a more readily identifiable link between the three sections, a presiding genius like Geoffrey Hill's Offa in his *Mercian Hymns*, 'overlord of the M5'. I cannot see, however, that such a narrative device would be possible here, or that Garner fails to make his themes clear by juxtaposition, by echoes of language, image and incident, and by providing his characters with a talisman and a territory which bind them together and establish a channel of communication between the three couples.

Perhaps the most important of the book's unifying concerns is astronomy, the stars with which Garner compared human emotion in . . . *All Systems Go* . . .. The red shift is an astronomical term, the significance of which, if I understand it correctly, is that it proves that the universe is expanding. Garner uses it as a symbol of isolation, emptiness and futility: the world is unknowable, the boundaries of knowledge are ever receding. Thomas needs a 'red shift' like Robert Fulleshurst, the last Roman Catholic incumbent of Barthomley church, in the stone folds of whose fifteenth-century funeral monument some pathetic tatters of scarlet still remain;[9] like Margery's petticoat, and the cars which Thomas sees in his delirium;[10] the red shift is ironically not only a desolating image but also an uplifting one, in the sense that Tom needs to shift his emotional spectrum away from 'the blues'. Tom is one of the modern men who in Giorgio de Santillana's words is 'unable to fit himself into the concepts of today's astrophysics short of schizophrenia'.

Santillana and von Deckend's thesis in *Hamlet's Mill* that astronomy is the 'main source of myth' is central to *Red Shift*, and their exposition of the intimate relationship between mill imagery and the heavens provides one of the novel's most striking images:[11] Mow Cop is 'the netherstone of the world. The skymill turns on it to grind the stars.' Mills and querns have been associated with the heavens because in their turning they symbolise the world axis, and the book's talismanic axe is thus incorporated in this image because it is connected both philologically (axe is derived ultimately from the Greek ἄξων, the axis of heaven)[12] and folkloristically, through the universal belief in such objects as thunderstones bringing good luck and protection from evil.[13]

The three stories are linked specifically by references to the star Delta Orionis: Macey identifies with it to stir himself into a frenzy; the rector asks John in the Civil War if he can 'loose the cords of Orion'; Tom and Jan look at it every night at 10.00 when they are apart. It is no accident that the Shakespeare sonnet (no. 116) from which Tom quotes twice is one in which love is compared to a star. Orion is a fool: R. H. Allen writes in *Star-names and their meanings*, 'we find in the various versions of the *Book of Job* and *Amos* the word Orion for the original Hebrew word kesīl, literally signifying "foolish", "impious", "inconstant", or "self-confident".' Allen also tells us that the Romans considered Orion unlucky.

When Tom and Jan decide on Delta Orionis as their private means of keeping in touch, Tom calls it 'a communications satellite'. As Margaret Esmonde observed in her excellent review of the book in *Fantasiae*, 'Garner expresses . . . isolation through a number of ironic symbols, . . . most of which are communication devices . . . television, tape-recorders and telephones.' A number of these communication devices are ones which disturb or counter the natural progression of time: Jan's parents' patients prefer to speak to an answering machine, and then have their problems played back; Tom can play and replay the tape of 'Cross Track' as often as he likes, though he uses the tape-recorder not to communicate but to withdraw; the wrestler who 'on every screen . . . bounced off the same ropes into the same forearm smash' was 'recorded last week'; when Tom and Jan look at their private satellite 'It's so far away, we're looking at it as it was when the Romans were here.' Only in the male characters' fits can the void be bridged: Macey cries out in his agony 'The distance is gone between us.'

One of the most impressive, and overlooked, achievements of the book is the air of solidity and verisimilitude which Garner imparts to his two historical episodes. The second and seventeenth centuries are as immediate and convincing as the twentieth. Although the Roman episode must be almost entirely a hypothetical imaginative re creation it is wholly believable, partly because of Garner's daring decision to invest his Roman soldiers, mostly Celts who have joined the Imperial army[14] but are now forced to go 'tribal' to survive in hostile country, with the manners and speech of American soldiers in Vietnam. As the Romans, apart from Logan, are not really Roman, so 'the Irish' in the Civil War strand of *Red Shift* are not really Irish.

Readers brought up on Rosemary Sutcliff do not expect to hear Roman soldiers deciding to 'hit the infrastructure', but this slang is much vivider than any more sober language. It makes the soldiers real, and provides a direct, violent, disturbing line from them to us, from then to now. It is a welcome change from the usual lacklustre imitations of Kipling and Sutcliff, though its self-conscious anachronism clashes with the scholarly re-creation of the Civil War episode.

F. H. Thompson writes in *Roman Cheshire* that 'the identity of the native inhabitants of Cheshire at the time of the Roman conquest presents a problem', and of the four possible tribes suggests as most likely a northern branch of the Cornovii. Garner posits the presence of two mutually antipathetic tribes, the Cornovii and the Brigantes, referred to, in a brilliant use of slang,[15] as the Cats and the Mothers. While the depiction of these tribes, about whom our information is severely limited, is, like the rest of Garner's picture of second-century Cheshire, necessarily built up from hints and hypotheses, it is artistically coherent and never jarringly unlikely. It is quite reasonable, too, to suggest that members of the Ninth legion might be in Cheshire after whatever disaster overtook it, as in the original Roman 'conquest' of Cheshire, again according to Thompson, 'the bulk of the campaigning . . . probably fell on the Ninth'.

Unstated in the *Red Shift* text, though inferable from it, is the premise that the remnants of the discredited Ninth Hispana have escaped while being marched north to work as labourers on Hadrian's wall (Hadrian is a 'minging stone-mason'), a story which has its basis in a fragment of oral lore collected by Garner after a performance of *Holly From the Bongs*:

> '. . . we were reviving somebody from the audience with hot soup when she said that her grandmother, who lived on Mow Cop, had always told a story about some Spanish slaves who were being marched north by the Romans to build a wall. The slaves had escaped and tried to settle on Mow Cop.'[16]

From this Garner extrapolated the megalomaniac figure of Logan, an insane Malebron, and his three Celtic companions, Face, Magoo and Macey. In the Vietnam analogy he found an image which could contain and refine the terror of the situation, men at the end of their tether. Garner's *Red Shift* research files contain numerous cuttings on My Lai, and a picture of three manic American soldiers dragging a dead comrade behind them. They are labelled Logan, Magoo, Macey.

It would be a mistake, however, to see the Roman soldiers simply as G.I.s. An analogy, not an identification, is made. The Roman massacre in Barthomley recalls not only My Lai but also the numerous similar massacres of Red Indians chronicled in Dee Brown's *Bury My Heart at Wounded Knee*, just as the Civil War Barthomley massacre echoes Dee Brown's description of the Wounded Knee outrage in 1890. According to Turning Hawk, a survivor of Wounded Knee, Black Coyote 'a crazy man, a young man of very bad influence and in fact a nobody' fired his gun into the air like Thomas Rowley and 'immediately the soldiers returned fire and indiscriminate killing followed'. Tom's copy of Dee Brown's book is deliberately visible in the *Red Shift* film.

The Barthomley massacre is well documented. The fullest and seemingly most trustworthy account is that of Thomas

Malbon, a Cheshire attorney (1577/8–1658), whose manuscript account of the Civil War has been printed by J. Hall.[17] It is on this that the more widely known and biased account of Edward Burghall is based. According to Malbon:

> 'The Kinges ptie. comynge to Barthomley Churche, did sett upon the same; wherein about XX^tie Neighbours where gonne for theire saufegarde. But *maior Connaught,* maior to *Colonel Sneyde,* (whom they in the Churche did take for the *Lord Brereton,*) wth his forces by wyelcome entred the Churche. The people w^thin gatt up into the Steeple; But the Enymy burnynge formes, pewes, Rushes & the lyke, did smother theim in the Steeple that they weire Enforced to call for quarter, & yelde theim selves; wch was graunted them by the said Connaught; But when hee had theim in his power, hee caused theim all to be stripped starke Naked; And moste barborouslie & contr'y to the Lawes of Armes, murthered, stabbed and cutt the Throats of xij of theim; viz: *m^r John ffowler* (Scholem^r), *Henry ffowler, m^r Thomas Elcocke, James Boughey, Randall Hassall, Richard Steele, & Richard Steele,* (bis.) *Will'm Steele, George Burrowes, Thomas Hollins, James Butler, & Richard Cawell*; & wounded all the reste, leavinge many of theim for Dead. And on Christmas daye, and S^te· Stevens Daye, the(y) Contynued plu'dringe & destroyinge all Barthomley, Crewe, Haslington, & the places adiacent takeing all theire goods, victualls, Clothes, and stripped many, bothe men & women, almost naked.'[18]

Readers of *Red Shift* will recognise in this the broad outlines of Garner's story, and also some of the names: John Fowler, Jim Boughey, Randal Hassall, Dick Steele. Garner also uses Burghall's account (Burghall calls John Fowler 'a hopeful young man',[19] the major in *Red Shift* calls him 'a most promising young man'), the supposed intercepted letter from 'that base and bloudy (pretended Lord) Sir *John Byrom*'[20] to the Marquess of Newcastle (dated Dec. 26 1643, and thought by J. Hall to be an early example of black propaganda; it is certainly a marked contrast to the tone of Byron's letter to the besieged inhabitants of Nantwich, quoted by Joseph Partridge)[21] and the fragments of oral tradition collected by Hinchliffe. When the major says of the slaughter 'It is the best way to proceed with their kind of people, for mercy to them is cruelty' he is closely paraphrasing a sentiment widely attributed to, if not actually held by, the man deemed responsible for the massacre.[22] According to Daniel Stringer, an inhabitant of Barthomley who was 97 when he was interviewed by Hinchliffe in 1839, and whose grandfather was one of the three men who escaped the scene unwounded, 'The son of the Rector fired from the steeple upon the troops marching past, and killed one of them; this so irritated the others, that they revenged his death by butchering many within the church.' This act of John Fowler's is transformed by Garner into his cruel taunting of Thomas, which provokes the fit in which he sets off his gun, firing, like Black Coyote, into the uninjurable sky.

Thomas Venables (another Thomas), the local man who kills John Fowler, rapes Margery and saves Thomas, is the only soldier known to have taken part in the massacre. His petition for a pension, mentioning his service at 'Bartomley', is in the Quarter Session Records for 1663. The Venables family is an old Cheshire one, and the story of how they acquired their land, around Moston, is, as Thomas says, of a dragon slaying.[23] The ancestor who killed the dragon by Bache Pool was another Thomas Venables. Venables' view of his family's heroic heritage is as bitter and ironic as his actions would lead us to suppose: 'Me grandfather, or some such, I don't know. Anyroad, he killed a dragon, they said, so they give him where it was at. Only because it's fit for nowt.'

Rudheath, to which Venables takes Thomas and Margery, where Tom lives and where Logan profanes the sacred snake, was a medieval sanctuary, one of three large secular sanctuaries in Cheshire in the Middle Ages.[24] By Tom's time, sanctuary has mutated to prison. Jan's house, standing on the border, offers hope even in its Latinate name, 'The Limes'.

The question of sanctuaries and sacred places, and how they retain or lose their apartness when no longer used for worship, recurs throughout the text. The shrine at Rudheath becomes a caravan site, a dead place; in the soulless centre of Crewe, Tom and Jan are 'at a precinct' (praecinctum implies a religious area); the church at Barthomley (which sports a 'cat-headed gargoyle' in remembrance of the Cornovii) becomes gradually secularised.

For Thomas and Margery, Mow Cop is the promise of peace after bloodshed and disaster, sanctuary; for Tom and Jan it is a special, private refuge; for the Cats, holy ground. One of the main concerns of *Red Shift* is to identify and define the sacramental. It does not refer directly to mythology, but instead seeks the central quality of myth, the quality of sacredness. In the Roman episode, two religious beliefs are quite thoroughly represented: the first, that of the Cats, an earth mother fertility cult which worships an incarnate corn goddess; the second, that of the Mothers, a violent, masculine cult of war and blood offerings. The Mothers worship a divine snake (to whom Magoo recites an incantation; Macey's similar 'big words' are Mithraic) to whom they offer a tribute of human heads. As Anne Ross writes 'the head was prized by the Celts as a war trophy . . . severed heads were impaled on stakes about their dwellings and temples.' The serpent was a symbol of the Celtic horned god.

Although it is impossible to accurately divide what we know about Celtic religion into specific cults, the violent horned god and the earth mother do seem to represent two ends of the same spectrum of belief. Not that the Cats spurn violence: all the Romans except Macey are ritually slaughtered for sleeping with the goddess; Macey is saved not only for his restraint, and not only because he is marked out by the gods, but also because he and the girl, as do Thomas and

97

Margery, eventually achieve a precarious balance in their love, of the sort which is denied to Tom and Jan.

The people of Barthomley in 1643 are Christian enough to seek refuge in the church, but not to turn the other cheek. In the battle for authority between the Fowlers it is the terrorist son John whom they follow to their cost, leaving Richard, the rector, mouthing prayers and sermons unheeded, and in his final despair returning (though this is not stated) to the Roman liturgy, an ironic reply to Jim Boughey's earlier comment as father and son swop Greek and Latin tags 'I like to hear the old church talk again.' All recognise Thomas' thunderstone as a sacred object. The idea of totem objects recurs throughout the book; ironically it is Jan, who scorns the woman she sees playing bingo with a lump of coal for a talisman, who sets most store by the axe-head, her 'Bunty'. In the contemporary story, the church has dwindled into somewhere to keep warm and eat sandwiches, and the rector into a man who must celebrate the rites alone, whose only acceptable face to Tom is that of the antiquarian and scholar, though Tom does recognise when he screams his pain that 'It needs a church'.

It is not Celtic cults or Christianity which provide the central religious focus of the book: it is individual, not communal, religious experience which Garner is primarily concerned to explore. Through the motif of the male characters' shared fits he considers the nature of godhead, and the possibility that man can not only approach but partake of the divine. Macey is possessed by a god, like the classic Icelandic berserk (Tom actually says 'I've gone berserk'; the word is also used, interestingly, by David of Findhorn); in the Civil War John Fowler anticipates Dostoievsky by several centuries in his attitude to Thomas' fits: 'that man sees God'. Margery's answer emphasises the ambivalence of such a gift: 'Him? Thomas? Where's God when you're stiff as a plank and your tongue's down your throat?' Tom seems cut off by his education from the ecstasy of his fits, aware only of the agony.

As usual in Garner's writing, education is seen, both for Tom and John, as isolating rather than liberating: in the final climactic scene between Tom and Jan on Mow Cop Tom is left helpless, mouthing quotations, pathetically unable to express himself, as he had been earlier in the argument with his parents. John Fowler's inability to, as he promises, 'find my own words' is realised in Tom.

A link can be drawn between Garner's interest in shamanism, illustrated both by *The Guizer* and 'Inner Time', and his treatment of Macey, Thomas and Tom. All three are, to differing extents, failed shamans,[25] men who have been unable to creatively master their illness and use it as an instrument of healing, social control and mediation between the physical and spirit worlds. In the introduction to *The Guizer* Garner writes that the guizer's 'shadow shapes the light'; Tom's 'giant shadow was on the wood outside, like a hole in space among the white birches'. These images in turn recall the description of the men of Elidor as they appear to Roland when he returns to Manchester to collect the treasures: 'They were becoming not shadows, but black holes in the air: holes in space.' All of the descriptions of the irruption of other-world beings into our world in Garner's work employ a linked imagery which eventually coalesces in this image of the black hole which may be either positive or negative. The Horsemen of Donn in *The Moon of Gomrath* chapter 3, the men from Elidor in *Elidor* chapters 9, 13 and 16, Gwyn going 'all shadowy' in *The Owl Service* chapter 3, the hut in *The Owl Service* chapter 11, after Gwyn sees Blodeuwedd, which is 'a black hole'; these incidents and others lie behind the description of Tom's shadow, and what it is saying both about the nature of his disturbance and his inability to deal with it.

In 'Inner Time' Garner speaks admiringly of societies in which epileptics and the mentally sick 'manifest their symptoms under the control of their will, in the service of the

community, to heal the sick and to communicate with God.'
Tom, however, is unable to be anything but destructive. The
first two relationships are relatively successful because the
men are still, if only subliminally, aware of the potential
beneficence of their affliction, and the women are still, if
clumsily, able to control it. Tom has no such awareness; Jan
seeks help outside the relationship, turning a precious, if
damaged, love affair into 'a case'.

The transcendent ecstatic experiences of Macey, Thomas
and Tom seem to posit 'the intersection of the timeless
moment'[26] as the source of conventional ideas of divinity.
Although John Fowler can claim that Thomas sees God, what
in fact he experiences seems to be a confused apprehension of
Tom; his ecstasy may be fundamentally religious, in the sense
that a true understanding of the nature of time may lead to a
reappraisal of those qualities of mind which have been
traditionally regarded as 'religious' or 'spiritual', but it is not
conventionally so.

Whether or not the ecstasies or fits experienced by the
characters constitute a withdrawal of the personality and the
substitution of some other awareness, or whether they
constitute the coexistence of individual and other aware-
nesses, or, as I think, merely a heightening, intensification or
liberation of ordinary consciousness is difficult to decide.
'Whether his soul were in or out of the body, he could not
tell.'[27] Both Susan and Alison, in previous books, become
vessels for supernatural power. Their own will to act and their
sense of identity are driven out or submerged, respectively by
the Brollachan and Blodeuwedd. While Gwyn and Roger may
be said to be the emotional counterparts of Llew and Gronw,
Alison *is* Blodeuwedd. Susan's descent into Abred and ascent
to the Region of the Summer Stars may be thought to parallel
the spirit journey undertaken by a shaman, but the resemblance is superficial, for the same reason that I call the characters
in *Red Shift* 'failed' shamans, because she is not in control.

The presentation of Tom's rages seems to suggest that they proceed from the confluence of an individual psychological upheaval with the energy inherited from analogous historical situations. The question of whether the earlier incidents should be seen as happening in the past or as coexistent, which has exercised many of Garner's critics, seems to me to be irrelevant here. What should be noted is that a preoccupation with timelessness is sustained by a rigorously accurate and specific reproduction of historical context. As regards the novel's view of time, I feel that it is not so much that time is thought to be ever present in the sense that there is no succession and no causality (as Walter McVitty, the book's most perceptive critic, puts it that '*It all exists at once*') but rather that Garner is supplying an affirmative answer to J. W. Dunne's theories in *An Experiment With Time*. Dunne asks whether 'the universe was, after all, really stretched out in Time, and that the lop-sided view we had of it – a view with the "future" part unaccountably missing, cut off from the growing "past" part by a travelling "present moment" – was due to a purely mentally imposed barrier which existed only when we were awake? So that, in reality, the associational network stretched not merely this way and that in Space, but also backwards and forwards in Time.' The barrier is suspended not only in dreams but in the characters' fits.

My use of the word 'rage' of Tom emphasises an important point about the 'ecstatic' experiences described in *Red Shift*, that they are closely associated with a sort of formless, frustrated anger. Macey's fits take the form of berserk violence; Thomas's more easily recognisable epilepsy is brought on by emotion which is violent both in form and content; Tom's disturbed behaviour follows emotional 'scenes' or sexual failure. The anger is to a large extent self-directed in each case: Macey feels helpless, a burden on his 'brilliant mates'; Thomas feels inferior to John Fowler and 'second-best' to Thomas Venables; Tom is obsessed by a sense of failure and inadequacy. Like Gwyn, who also runs to a sink in a state of extreme emotion, Tom has 'a chip on his shoulder a mile high'; in his case transcendent experience has degenerated into sulkiness. As Marghanita Laski points out, 'there . . . seem to be several resemblances between outbursts of anger and intensity ecstasies.'[28]

The fits of the main characters are not moments of joyful union with God, of oneness with the universe; they experience no enlarging of consciousness, no momentary lucidity or clarity, no regenerative vision, except in the sense that it is only in their fits that they are fully and clearly aware of their isolation, their confusion and their uncertainty. Because they are not joyful ecstatics they are vouchsafed no revelation. Each of them could say with Huw 'I don't know what I know.'

It may not be too outrageous to suggest that Garner sees his own function as author as in some ways akin to that of the shaman;[29] his ritualised exorcisms of what, in 'Inner Time', he calls 'engrams' (engrained psychological scars which become harmfully incorporated into habitual patterns of thought and behaviour) can be equated with shamanistic 'trips', which are not only self-purifying but also involve the audience/reader in the reliving, reordering and resolution of 'tensions, fears and conflicts'[30] at deep psychological levels. Certainly he sees the supernatural in practical terms far removed from the fey mysticism of so many children's writers, postulating a real and manipulable connection between man and the forces of nature: the moon, which is the source of the 'old magic' in *The Moon of Gomrath*; the heavens, which supply the talismanic 'thunderstone' and the pervasive star imagery of *Red Shift*; and, most important, the land. He needs, he told Iain Finlayson in 1977, 'to partake of it as it partakes of me almost in a Eucharistic sense'.

In suggesting that Garner is in his books both reliving and relieving intense personal experiences, in a sense his own psychic history, I do not wish to imply that he is a confessional writer. His own catharsis, if such it is, occurs at a submerged level. By means of his increasingly adept manipulation of traditional material Garner distances his books from the private concerns which they express, and instead involves the reader in an analogous spiritual journey. Like the shaman, Garner comes to terms with his private pain in private; in public he is the healer and mediator. The reader is not expected to be a spectator at Garner's public self-revelation or self-examination, but is required to respond actively to dilemmas which are not simply personal but universal, to participate. The 'difficulty' of his books is most apparent to those who resist the necessary personal involvement.

Garner continually stresses, as to Finlayson, that 'It is not confessional writing'. In his painfully frank ICA lecture 'Inner Time' he enlarges on this, in the context of his idea of art as the discharging of engrams. An engram is a sort of reaction on ice, 'a memory-trace, a permanent impression made by a stimulus or experience', and may be either acquired or inherited (as the 'collective unconscious'). In this definition myth is seen as the accumulation of man's psychic traumas, in Garner's 1970 words 'distilled and violent truth . . . spiritual gelignite', interpreted through the individual's own experience. Mental illness is caused by damaging engrams, creative energy 'imploding', and can thus be harnessed to the will, causing the gelignite to explode creatively rather than implode destructively. He writes in 'Inner Time': 'The discharge of an engram through writing may be an act of exorcism, but it is not confessional writing. If it succeeds, I am not giving the reader the burden of my engram, but I am fortuitously handing on the unreleased, and thereby refined and untainted, energy.'

'Inner Time' gives a number of insights into Garner's method and ideas in writing *Red Shift*. Describing the process of exorcising pain in psychoanalysis by constant rehearsal of engrams, he writes that 'the usual pattern is to move from historical event to historical event, sometimes taking shortcuts through truth and dream'. Similarly, when differentiating between 'inner' and 'outer' time, he writes that

> 'All events seem to be simultaneously present: only our immediate needs give an apparent perspective. We can check the validity of this argument by calling to mind any two intensely remembered experiences. They will be emotionally contemporaneous, even though we know that the calendar separates them by years. Similarly, it is possible to reverse the calendar by comparing emotions which are not of equal strength.'

The lecture confirms, as one would expect from his work, that what is most important to Garner is an awareness of the interaction of experiences, of the web which binds each incident, each word, each life inextricably together.

Although Garner clarifies much of his intention in *Red Shift* in 'Inner Time', his statement that the basic 'myth' of which it is an expression is 'the story of Tamlain and Burd Janet and the Queen of Elfland' is hard to accept. One of the strands of the contemporary story is certainly Tom's need for Jan to hold on to him, whatever monstrous shape he may assume, and so free him from the domination of his small-minded mother, whose inhibiting possessiveness seems likely to make him a 'tiend to hell'[31] rather than allow him to fulfil his intellectual and emotional promise. All three men are to some extent in thrall to the unearthly, in their uncontrollable fits, and need to be saved by instinctive, unreserved female love; all three of them at various points need to be held and mothered; it is possible, though until I attempted to make the story of *Red Shift* conform to that of 'Tam Lin' it had not occurred to me, that we are to assume that Jan is pregnant at the end of the book, as the girl is and Margery may be. If this is so, in all three cases the man would be only a putative or substitute father: Macey's brilliant mates have fathered the girl's child in their brutal assault; Margery, if she is pregnant, may well be so by Thomas Venables not Thomas Rowley ('It's all right, I mean, same as, if you are'); although Tom would be the actual father of any child of Jan's, he would feel usurped by the German wine-grower whose seduction of her is the ostensible cause of Tom's anguish.[32] However, I must admit that I find the connection between 'Tam Lin' and *Red Shift* tenuous; without being told to do so, I doubt if many people would make it. Certainly we do not find in *Red Shift* a straightforward use of 'Tam Lin' to provide a symbolism of psychological withdrawal and the need to be loved 'for better or for worse' in anything like the same sense that we do in Catherine Storr's *Thursday*.[33]

The literary work to which *Red Shift* most consistently refers is *King Lear*, not 'Tam Lin'. Both Tom and Macey persistently refer to the mad scene of *Lear* and, by doing so, of course, to Child Roland. Tom's insistent 'Tom's a cold', the key he impresses so fervently on Jan at their last meeting, has echoes, too, of Balurdo's 'I am acolde' at the close of Marston's *Antonio's Revenge*, linking the climax of *Red Shift* with that of *Elidor*.

Other quotations are less obviously apt: it is difficult to account specifically for the narrator's early ironic defacement of Tennyson's

> *'On one side lay the Ocean, and on one*
> *Lay a great water, and the moon was full'*

('On one side lay the M6, and on one lay a great water. and the site was full'; there is also an echo of *The Weirdstone of Brisingamen* chapter 1 'On one side lay the fields, and on the other the steep slopes'), though this whole scene uses quotations to emphasise the inhibition of Tom's emotions by his intellect. The proverb borrowed from Masefield's *The Box of Delights*, 'More know Tom Fool than Tom Fool knows', is a key text.

As far as Garner's own work is concerned, *Red Shift* is most fully linked with *Elidor*: by their mutual climactic reference to

Marston, by Thomas' name, Rowley, by the dark tower imagery applied to Barthomley Church, and by Garner's vision of modern England as a wasteland; though in *Red Shift*, as Margaret Esmonde points out, 'no golden land is glimpsed to comfort the protagonist'. Tom, like Roland, is 'not safe loose.'

The style of *Red Shift* is essentially an extension and refinement of that employed in *The Owl Service*: clipped, allusive, ruthlessly pared down, yet dense. It is a complex of unresolved tensions from which clear, simple statements emerge, large and uncluttered, by a curious teasing of the reader's creative sympathy. The text is bare, shorn of all extraneous comment, and the narrative voice modulates in accordance with necessity. Sometimes the narrative persona approximates to Tom (or Macey, Thomas, Margery or John); sometimes the perspective shifts into pure description.

We are always aware of a mesh of consciousness, which thickens or separates at various points as the narrative focus adjusts, through which the dialogue is being filtered. In an article written in 1968, 'The Best of Garner', Patrick Richardson had already noted the influence of Pinter on *Elidor*. In *Red Shift*, the influence of Pinter and Beckett (according to Michael Moynihan, again writing in 1968, 'the only writer he wholly admires') is all-pervasive, and the resulting dialogue is taut and incisive, with the edge of a casual knife thrust. One of *Red Shift*'s reviewers, John Winton, in an attempt to denigrate the book, which he violently disliked, perceived, despite himself, the dialogue's quality: 'These lines are how ordinary chat would appear, if it were orchestrated like chamber music.'

What is interesting about this technique is how much it enables Garner to communicate without ever expressing it in words. The whole of Tom and Jan's sexual relationship, for instance, is contained in the pauses between sentences. It is quite clear, but it is neither described nor mentioned. John

Berger's 1968 article 'Writing a love scene' is important in this context, both because it speaks out eloquently against the overt portrayal of sexual experience in art, and because it does so in the context of an argument about the uncommunicable quality of 'firstness' in the sexual act which is closely allied to Eliade's thinking about myth and time, and hence with *Red Shift*'s larger cosmological preoccupations. Narrative, Berger argues, automatically both implies a voyeur and puts an experience in the past tense, both of which inevitably turn any description of sexual activity into the description of acts rather than experiences, and hence into lies. Garner's avoidance of direct description here is not simply a technical trick, and certainly not a sop to a child audience: it is a restatement of one of the book's major themes, of the incompatability of the inner and outer worlds.

At first sight *Red Shift* reads like a film script: the action proceeds almost wholly by dialogue, the narrative cuts from scene to scene without apology or explanation, and in his three versions of the scene in Barthomley Church when John taunts Thomas about Margery's previous suitor he treats reality with the contempt for objective truth that film has given us. The differences between Thomas, John and Margery's perceptions of the scene illuminate the book's central preoccupation with the difficulties of communication, and may also point to a solution of the book's problems. Singly, the characters are lost; together, they form a whole. 'I'm not completed, Madge. I'll say it now. You and I meet in Thomas.'

In 1974, acknowledging the influence of Japanese legends on his work, Garner went on to say that 'I'm influenced even more by Japanese films. You could play an amusing game by seeing how many times in each book I milk *Seven Samurai*. And in *Red Shift*, for instance, the death of Magoo is the climax of *Throne of Blood*.'[34] The influence of film on Garner's technique and content is undoubtedly large: the villagers' taunting of Nancy in *The Owl Service*, for instance, derives from Emlyn Williams' *The Last Days of Dolwyn*.

However, a comparison of one's experience of the book with the film made of *Red Shift* for the BBC's 'Play for Today' series in 1977 emphasises the importance of its literary rather than cinematic qualities. There is not a sense in the book of a missing element, as there is in a printed film script; the book is a literary exploitation of cinematic convention, but the idea that the result of that exploitation resembles a cinematic experience is an illusion, and, as such, evidence of the literary success of the technique. The texture of *Red Shift* is in fact too dense, too condensed, to transfer happily, or intact, to the screen (which is not to deny the film of *Red Shift* its own virtues; but, whatever these are, they are not so nearly those of the book as was the case in the film of *The Owl Service*). Take, for instance, the climax of the book's opening scene between Tom and Jan: in a handful of lines a picture is painted which is absolutely clear, both visually and emotionally, but which it would be impossible to translate onto film with anything like the same economy or effectiveness. That first image, while precise and comprehensible, only *feels* cinematic:

> 'The motorway roared silently.[35] Birds skittered the water in flight to more distant reeds, and the iron water lay again, flat light reflecting no sky. The caravans and the birches. Tom.
> "Next week," said Jan. "Right?" Her knuckles were comfortless between his. "Next week. I go next week." She tried to reach the pain, but his eyes would not let her in.
> "London?"
> "Yes." Teeth showing through lips drawn: lines from sides of nostrils: frown and pain lines. "And my parents —".'

The film, which was completely rethought (although not, in the end, radically different from the book) does not seem to me to adequately contain the violence of the book, despite the highly professional standard of its making, and the occasional inspired touch such as the slivers of glass when Tom breaks the window turning into the spears slicing through the tent towards Macey, or the attempt to assimilate the noise of the motorway to Macey's cries and the drawing of swords in the seventeenth century. The film is too compressed, and has no time to develop a comparably subtle system to replace the book's delicate tissue of verbal cross-reference. Similarly, the camera is not flexible enough to sustain the role previously borne by the novel's variable narrative voice.

In the end the film is interesting more as a further comment on the novel than as a separate artistic achievement. It stresses, for instance, the resemblance to Tom of both John Fowler and Face, and clarifies the fact that the characters' visions are only of the future, so that both film and book could be said to be dreamed or related by Macey or his alter ego; at the end of the book, Macey's ' "I'll watch," he said. "Bluesilvers. It might matter." ' identifies Macey's voice with the narrator in the final 'It doesn't matter'; though that voice is triune.

Whether or not *Red Shift* is a children's book will no doubt remain a matter of controversy; it is a question I cannot solve. It is a book about negative energy, and seems to me to be an adolescent document in the same sense as *Romeo and Juliet*; the tendency of reviewers to refer to Tom and Jan as 'star-crossed lovers' is perhaps a recognition of this. It is not, however, an entirely despairing book. Tom and Jan are not the only couple in the book, and the happiness or at least survival of both Macey and the girl and Thomas and Margery is implicit in the survival of the axe. Tom and Jan have neither the information nor the maturity to cope with their unhappiness, but in the end it is only Tom who is irreparably damaged. If we accept for a moment Garner's view of *Elidor*, we can see that the ending of *Red Shift* is neither more nor less nihilistic or despairing than those of the previous two books. Garner was simply not allowing his central characters to survive.

6

The Tom and Jan couple had already appeared in Garner's writing before *Red Shift* under other names, in his 1966 short story 'Feel Free' and his 1964 radio play 'In Case of Emergency', and were to make one more desultory appearance, though this time with a happy ending, in his slight 1979 TV play *Lamaload*.

Lamaload, the story of a girl's return with her boyfriend to her childhood home only to discover it has been turned into a reservoir, is beautifully shot (it was part of a series with the generic title 'A Sense of Place') but its message of the redemptive power of love, with David beating the landscape in a struggle for Jane's affections, is somewhat laboured. The play is interesting in that the Tom part is here taken by the girl and the Jan part by the boy but otherwise it is a trivial piece, memorable only for the moving visual reference to Garner's *Moon of Gomrath/Elidor* Grail imagery in the scene of Jane drinking water in her cupped hand from the stream which runs from her ruined home to the reservoir.

In Case of Emergency, which was published as a short story in 1967, starts as a comedy about the tensions of exclusive and excluding love relationships and ends as a horror story, as the two lovers get stuck with a large number of parcels in a telephone box, unable to escape. The phone box becomes a coffin: yet another communication device used to isolate or trap, just as Harry in *To Kill a King* is trapped as an image on his own television screen, and taunted by his word processor. The Tom character muses: 'All that space. And all that distance going past. And you're one human being in it. It seems impossible that I could ever find that bit of space you fill ever again.'

'Feel Free', which exists both as a story and as a film script, is more substantial; it is clearly a trial run for *Red Shift* in several senses, and its title resurfaces in *Red Shift*'s text when Face invites Logan to rape the Barthomley girl. It is Garner's only important piece of original imaginative prose writing outside his novels.

The story is simple: Brian is copying a Greek vase, which bears a picture of Charon ferrying a soul across Acheron, for a school project. He feels an immense, inexplicable closeness to the Greek potter, whose scarred thumbprint, preserved on the vase's base, is, but for the scar, the twin of his own. Brian takes Sandra to the Open Day at a new Holiday Camp, talking excitedly about his discoveries: the vase is (like books) a time capsule, fashioned with a purpose like the bottles full of bits and pieces Brian buried for posterity as a child: 'There's bits of you in the bottle, waiting all this time, see, in the dark, and as soon as the bottle's opened – time's nothing.' There is no gap between Brian and the Greek potter: they are contemporaneous, for every moment holds in it the promise of all others. As Tosh, the museum caretaker, puts it: 'They had time in them days. They had all the time there was. All the time in the world.'

'Feel Free' is more overtly supernatural than *Red Shift*; the end hints at some sort of time slip. As Brian disappears into the Tunnel of Love, his thumb burning from the gash which has joined him to the potter, Sandra's question 'Shall I see you next time round?' expects the answer no.

Like *The Moon of Gomrath* and *Elidor*, 'Feel Free' is in two parts, in the museum and the Lay-Say-Fair Holiday Camp, which fit uncomfortably together, but the themes of craftsmanship and the manipulability of time are handled with great skill, and the three figures of Brian, Tosh and Sandra are brought convincingly to life. Set against the soulless plasticity of the Holiday Camp Brian and Sandra's relationship has a pleasing vibrancy. The main conclusion is clear: when human beings connect, 'time's nothing'.

Brian and Sandra are a less troubled, less intelligent couple than Tom and Jan, and, inevitably in a short story, less complex. They are, however, clearly intimately related to the later pair; particularly Brian, whose thoughtfulness, punning humour and sardonic perceptiveness are also Tom's.

If 'Feel Free' represents an important step towards a realisation of the themes and characters of *Red Shift*, *The Guizer* is *Red Shift*'s companion volume. It is recognizably a product of the same artistic impulse, and its bibliography and contents provide one key to the novel's mysteries. The extraordinary graffito on the title page, a sun hero whose left hand traces the name Tom by his side, leaves one in no doubt that the two works are closely connected. *The Guizer* is an important book, with a central focus that *The Hamish Hamilton Book of Goblins* lacked. It illuminates *Red Shift*, casts a certain amount of light on *Elidor*, *The Owl Service* and even the first two novels, and, what is more, amounts to a powerful statement about the quality in myth which attracts its compiler. The stories vary widely in time and culture, but they are all attempts to define a dimension somehow beyond but inextricably part of the human; the area which Garner defines in his introduction as 'the dawning godhead in Man'.

A guizer is literally an actor in a mumming play or folk ritual; Garner uses it as a synonym for trickster. The element of Fool, he writes in his introduction, 'is where our humanity lies'. 'The fool is the advocate of uncertainty: he is at once creator and destroyer, bringer of help and harm. He draws a boundary for chaos, so that we can make sense of the rest. He is the shadow that shapes the light.' To a certain extent Garner sems to see the Guizer as the creator, the author.

The book is in three sections, loosely considering the Guizer as Fool, Man and God, in an attempt to reproduce with sophisticated tales from many cultures something of the structure of the primitive trickster cycle as revealed by Radin, and by doing so to give back meaning to a form, the retold folktale or myth, which has been progressively debased, trivialised and undermined. The care with which Garner chose and arranged the stories in *The Guizer*, and the sensitive concern he shows in preserving the 'volatile essence of the storyteller', makes the book succeed not only on the level of the individual story but as a whole, as a coherent statement about the nature of the material. He skilfully avoids the danger which the resolution of many stories into a monolithic framework inevitably brings, that of producing a simplistic whole which concentrates on the archetypal at the expense of the ectypal. An archetype can only be the hard core around which what is individually worth while in each tale must be built, and Garner recognises this.

Like its author, I am reluctant to expound a 'meaning' for *The Guizer*, or to attempt to explain its shape. The following paragraphs are one reaction to the book, my own, not a recipe to be followed when reading it.

Part one, which Garner characterises as 'The Guizer as Fool', considers the animal element in man's nature. Many of the actors in the stories are part animal, part human, mummers in animal masks: Chulyen the crow, Ananse the spider, the Lad of the Skin Coverings. In the early anecdotes, such as 'The Astick Cuckoo' and 'Happy Boz'll', man has not learned either to understand or control the animals. He has, in 'The Smart Man and the Fool', learned to eat them, but they, if only in jest, have also learnt, in 'The Cow that Ate the Piper', to feed on him. Only when the hero Finn has overcome the Cu Glas are we ready to move on to the book's second section, which deals with 'the Guizer as Man'. We leave Finn asleep beneath the Smith's Rock at Skye, to wake in new birth in 'Tondi'.

Pitiful Oneside in this Batak fable recalls the man 'with one eye, one ear, one hand, and one foot' who escapes the Big Lad's wrath in 'The Lad of the Skin Coverings'. Man's portion is death, greed and lust; only a sort of combative innocence (in 'The Astick Pool', 'The Clerk of Barthomley') and an ability to rise beyond ourselves, so that Magtelt in 'Sir Halewyn' can become 'the Virgin without pity', can save us. Only by submitting to foolishness, to 'mad prankes, and merry Jestes', can we learn wisdom; only by the exercise of imagination gain entry to fairyland, where 'did King Oberon shew Robin Good-fellow many secrets, which hee never did open to the world'. The two long stories in this section, 'Sir Halewyn' and 'Robin Good-fellow' counterbalance each other. The one is a dark, the other a beneficent application of supernatural power, and their form is similar. It is no coincidence that Siewert Halewyn's arms are the crow; he is Chulyen before 'he began to feel sorry', and he is also Crow, the savage trickster hero of Ted Hughes' poetic cycle, and Thomas Venables, who appears to Margery 'like a crow above her head'. Robin Good-fellow, for all his mischief, is, as his name suggests, kindly inclined; but he still retains an ability to transform himself into animal shape. The recurrence of violent rape as a theme in these stories in part two of *The Guizer*, in 'Bobby Rag', 'Sir Halewyn' and 'Robin Good-fellow', forms a clear connection with *Red Shift*.

In part three, the Guizer achieves apotheosis. The graffito which precedes the texts retains only an attenuated, tenuous link with the physical man, and the chilling little verse which opens this final third,

> *'Under the earth I go,*
> *On the oak leaf I stand,*
> *I ride on the filly that never was foaled,*
> *And I carry the dead in my hand',*

prepares the reader for the strange journeys of Maui, the Red King's son and Hare. In each of these stories the hero is finally forced to submit to the inevitability of death, just as 'Number Eleven' fails to kill death in 'Spider-Stories'; in each of them, as in the final proverb, the finality, the absoluteness of death is questioned.

The cruelties and stupidities of the trickster are essentially redemptive, as the tentative identification of Hare with Christ in the introduction indicates. The book stops at the point where Hare and Christ merge, where the godhead in man ceases to be dawning and is fully realised. Only in the Ila proverb with which the book ends, 'A man does not die, except at the hour of his birth', and the endless knot of the swastika pelta graffito which follows it, is the book's 'message' made clear.

It would be nonsense to pretend that the structure of *The Guizer* is anything other than tentative and general. As Garner puts it in his introduction, each section has 'its own tendency', but there is no argument beyond the stories to which the book could be reduced. The structure borrowed from Radin's interpretation of the Winnebago trickster cycle is a source of inner strength, but it never dominates the individual stories. It is in the variety of representations of the trickster that the delight lies, not in the stories' subservience to a prearranged pattern, and it is the high quality of the stories as stories which makes them memorable. Trickster, the spirit Jung, with profound implications for Garner's imagery, termed 'shadow', represents in Garner's work the positive or negative application of mental disturbance: Robin Good-fellow or Sir Halewyn.

In the revised introduction to the paperback edition of *The Guizer* Garner claims Tom and Jerry cartoons as today's embodiment of trickster, and there is a clear link here with the subversive world of comics such as *The Beano* and *The Dandy* which Garner has often, as in his interview with Aidan

Chambers, identified as an important element of his imagination. It is in his concern with trickster that the influence of these comics is most strongly felt, but there are also direct echoes. The 'candle in darkness' which Roland sees and the black searchlight which leaps from the Mound of Vandwy, for instance, both recall the 'candle of darkness' which appeared in the 1942 Dandy serial 'The Magic Box'.

Garner's editorial policy in *The Guizer* is much as in *The Hamish Hamilton Book of Goblins*: such changes as are made are made to free the tongue of the original storyteller from fetters imposed in earlier translation or in the journey from the mouth to the page. In general, the stories are altered very little; the creative effort is in the compilation, the ordering and juxtaposition of the stories, as much as in the retelling. Only one group of changes is made for a less defensible reason than the struggle for clarity: the convention that such volumes are published for the young forces Garner to bowdlerise his opening story (though the details excised are scarcely missed) and to omit sections 15 and 16 of 'Hare'.

The five short humorous tales, 'The Big Stone', 'Turncoat' and the three Astick stories, are entirely rewritten; the only long story to be similarly treated is 'The Young Man, the Lion and the Yellow-Flowered Zwart-Storm Tree', which is retold from a literal translation which inevitably lacks the fluency and verbal control necessary in a story told for entertainment rather than scholarship. Often alterations amount to no more than a few native words translated into English in 'Chulyen', reparagraphing, shortening (as in 'Robin Good-fellow'), reversion to the literal meanings of Gaelic terms in 'The Lad of the Skin Coverings' (and native exclamations in 'Spider-Stories'), or the correction of obscurities in the sources ('Their fingers were like the prongs of wooden grapes', in 'The Smith's Rock in the Isle of Skye', becomes 'Their fingers were long like the tines of big rakes'). The dialect of 'Bobby Rag' is simplified for intelligibility, though Garner retains enough of its idiosyncrasy ('sneks' for 'snakes') to delight without confusing. In 'Foka' two stories are elided, with a final cap from yet a third place in Garner's source (unfortunately the word 'glass' in the original's 'great glass castles which incessantly turn and spin', with its Celtic and Arthurian overtones, is omitted on *The Guizer* p. 170, undoubtedly in error as 'glass' does appear on p. 172, and Garner refers to it in his note on the story); in 'Leza the Besetting One' three stories are joined together. Often nineteenth-century literary translations are softened to approach the colloquial: verbs are contracted, scholarly words replaced by common ones. In 'The Smart Man and the Fool', 'You eat and eat unto repletion' is replaced by 'You eat, eat, eat until you're sick'; in 'Turncoat', 'And the quondam chums fought' becomes 'And they began to fight'; in 'Spider-Stories' (in which Garner generally stays very close to Rattray's text) the coy 'and he made water over Death' is strengthened to 'and he pissed on Death'. The terseness of 'Tondi' is Garner's, as is the sonorous addition of the Batak triple god's name, 'Bataraguru, Sori, Balabulan', but the typically Garner sentences of some of the other stories are the result of his choosing stories which reflect his own style rather than of any drastic refashioning. In 'Maui-of-a-Thousand-Tricks', 'It flamed. Fire was.' is Alpers, not Garner.

The humorous tales, though slight, are important to the book, for they reinforce the deliberate irreverence of many of the longer stories. Much of the book's ability to engage the reader derives, as Eva Gillies noted in her perceptive review 'The Timeless Fool', from our 'cultural taboo against associating the comic too closely with the sacred'. These short, humorous tales are deceptively direct and rough-hewn: they are highly wrought pieces of prose. Garner reclaims their comic value by locating then in his own known territory of Cheshire: in 'Turncoat' instead of Dennett's 'they had made their farms close to one another' we have 'they had made their fields next neighbours'; 'The Big Stone' retains the kernel of MacCulloch's dry anecdote but completely refurbishes it with the vivid expressions of Cheshire dialect. These two stories and the Astick tales are interesting also as linguistic forerunners of the *Stone Book* quartet. They were written, Garner tells us in his notes, with the speech patterns of Wilf Lancaster of Swettenham (the miller who is featured in . . . *All Systems Go* . . . and *Images*) in mind, and these speech patterns can be heard again in the quartet. In 'The Astick Cuckoo', for instance, 'they'd half mauled themselves to death with raunging the stones'.

The important point about *The Guizer* is that it *is* a journey from 'the inchoate Wakdjungkaga to the self-knowledge of Hare'. It presents the instinctual life as in some ways beneficial but also cruel, wayward, ruthless, haphazard. Instinct must be dominated and ordered by intelligence. *The Guizer* is an expression of the respect for intelligence which accompanies in Garner's work the insistence that without instinct it is a sterile and dehumanising force. We can neither deny nor destroy instinct, only turn it towards good or evil, help or harm, 'blysse' or 'blunder'. The story of *The Guizer* is the story of man's growing ability to distinguish and choose between these opposites.

The Guizer was continued in Garner's next major folktale project, *The Lad of the Gad*, though here he focused on one culture, the Celtic one which had already provided several stories in both his previous collections. The stories' heroes are modified trickster figures: they make their own destinies, though they are never totally in control. Again, they seem almost an image of the artist. Certainly, the picture of Conal Crovi 'when the steak was coming out of me' recalls not only the similar situation in 'Bash Tchelik' in *Goblins* but also Garner's own statement in 'Coming to Terms' that in writing a book 'I have cut a piece of me off'.

The first four tales, 'Upright John', 'Rascally Tag', 'Olioll

Olom' and 'The Lad of the Gad', are all Scottish, and all taken from Campbell's *Popular Tales of the West Highlands*, the most important Celtic influence on Garner's early work. In them Garner keeps as close as he can to Campbell's inspired translations, making only those changes necessary to transform an oral text (Campbell's Gaelic texts were noted down word for word from storytellers working in an unbroken oral tradition) into a written one, in order to recreate for a literary audience the power the stories held for a non-literate one. The fifth story, in which the linguistic and plot strands of the first four are deftly knitted together, is based on the confused and dull Irish manuscript tale 'The Adventure of the Children of the King of Norway' translated by Douglas Hyde in the first volume of the Irish Texts Society.

In his story 'How Finn Maccumhail was in the House of the Rowan Tree without Power to Stand or Leave to Sit Down' in William Mayne's *The Hamish Hamilton Book of Heroes*, Garner had already shown himself a master at capturing Gaelic idiom and rhythms in English, but 'Lurga Lom' still represents a great achievement. The source is muddy and clogged; Garner's story is clear and lucent. Hyde's translation provides a skeleton and a few phrases, but the verbal felicities and the essence of the tale are supplied, or rediscovered, by Garner. The long digressive episode featuring Buinne Rough-Strong is omitted, with one of his adventures transferred to Lusca (Hyde's Cod), and the fact that the woman Eiteall at the end of the story is really Faylinn made clear.

The stories in *The Lad of the Gad* are violent, basic, raw. They are such tales as Child Roland might have heard in the Dark Tower. The extreme sensuousness of their imagery and the intricacy of their structure make them difficult to follow or appreciate on a first reading, but they well repay the reader's perseverance. Singly, they may seem over-rich and over-worked; together they possess the imagination with their urgent, inexpressible logic. For instance, 'Rascally Tag' when printed unedited in *Jubilee Jackanory* seemed confused and confusing; the other four stories in *The Lad of the Gad* set it in context.

Though sense may seem on a first reading to be subordinated to sound, the sense is there. They are quest tales, and the heroes are in search of power, of liberty, and, paradoxically in such harsh, masculine tales, of their own femininity, the denial of which cost Roland, Gwyn and Tom so dear. Mercy and pity are the messages derived from savagery, and those who refuse to acknowledge them, such as the slim, swarthy Champion, are savaged in their turn.

The last story, 'Lurga Lom', following on from 'The Lad of the Gad', is an account of a quest in search of the feminine principle: 'the Great Dug of the World', in contrast to the image of 'death's mouldy tits' at the close of Ted Hughes' *Crow*. *The Lad of the Gad*, like *The Guizer*, is to some extent a positive reaction to Hughes' negative trickster cycle in *Crow*. The hag/maiden who wields the Great Dug in 'Lurga Lom' and 'The Lad of the Gad' is also the Lady of the Green Isle in 'The Lad of the Skin Coverings' in *The Guizer*, and all the women in Garner's earlier books. Garner had already used the Great Dug image, which he introduces to the stories, in an ironic reversal in his comic operetta *The Belly-Bag*, based on a medieval tale, in which a witch employs a magical gourd to suck milk from cows.

One of the most attractive features of the stories is their repetitive, incantatory, ritualistic texture, noticeable in the repeated 'runs', a narrative device peculiar to the Gaelic hero tale, and the evocative opening and closing formulae. All four tales from Campbell open with the words 'There was a king' and end with sometimes incomprehensible traditional closures as satisfying as the last hammer blow which drives a nail exactly into position: 'And Olliol Olom made a wedding that night for his three daughters; leeg, leeg and beeg, beeg; solid sound and peg-drawing, gold crushing from the soles of their feet, the length of seven days and seven years.'

The first story, 'Upright John' from Campbell's 'MacIain Direach', is essentially the same story as the Grimms' 'The Golden Bird'. Another Celtic version of the story, from Kennedy's *Fireside Stories*, 'The Greek Princess and the Young Gardener', is given in Jacobs' *More Celtic Tales*. 'Upright John' is slightly condensed but keeps close to Campbell's text, drawing, as do the other stories, on his variants and notes (the name 'Bad Straddling Queen', for instance, is from a fragment printed in the notes; 'A man is kind to his life' is from Campbell's second version, 'Ai Sionnach, the Fox') and replacing any stiff or archaic phrases. There is also a continual heightening of language: 'out of sight of land' becomes 'making sea-hiding'; the Foxy Lad (in Campbell 'the Gille Mairtean') makes a 'dark spring'; the story of his encounter with the Giant of the Five Heads, the Five Humps and the Five Throttles is embroidered to great effect.

The second story, 'Rascally Tag', combines Campbell's two versions of 'The Slim Swarthy Champion'; Jacobs used them to supplement 'The Story Teller at Fault', the tale he took from Griffin's *Talis Qualis, or, Tales of the Jury Room* for *Celtic Fairy Tales*. To see what a beneficial change Garner has wrought in the story simply by adding a little of 'The History of the Ceabharnach' to 'The Slim, Swarthy Champion', adding a few touches, leaving out one or two dreary or tangled paragraphs, transferring Rascally Tag to a place of honour and refashioning the end is to realise how adept he is at recovering the essence of a tale.

'Olliol Olom', the third story, is mostly Campbell's 'The Tale of Conall Crovi'. Another version of the same story from Campbell, 'Conall Cra Bhuidhe', is given by Jacobs in *Celtic Fairy Tales* as 'Conall Yellowclaw'; an Irish version is given in *The Red Fairy Book*. The sea 'run' is from Campbell's

'Murachadh MacBrian'; the ending from 'The Brown Bear of the Green Glen'.

'The Lad of the Gad' is Campbell's 'The Knight of the Red Shield'. Again Garner condenses, trims, sharpens, but closely follows his source. The opening is from the notes to 'MacIain Direach'. The excellence of Garner's changes can easily be illustrated: Campbell's 'they drew the speckled barge up her own seven lengths on grey grass, with her mouth under her, where the scholars of a big town could neither make ridicule, scoffing or mockery of her', becomes 'they drew up the painted ship, the proud woman, her own seven lengths on grey grass, with her mouth under her'. Simply by moving a preposition, substituting 'painted ship' for 'speckled barge', omitting the redundant second half of Campbell's sentence and adding the words 'the proud woman' he has produced an image as sharp and incisive as a medieval miniature.

In general, his practice with these tales from Campbell is clear. He breaks up Campbell's long paragraphs, condenses phraseology and in some cases incident, tries to preserve the stories' uniquely Gaelic flavour and turns reported into direct speech. His success can be gauged by comparing his stories with Campbell's, or with the versions of 'The Knight of the Red Shield' and 'MacIain Direach' given in Iris MacFarlane's *The Mouth of the Night*, or the version of the latter in Norah and William Montgomerie's *The Well at the World's End*.

In 'Lurga Lom' (which Garner also used as the basis of a play/screenplay in which he explored the nature of the present violent conflict in Northern Ireland through the violence of the Irish saga) the four tales find resolution, and verbal elements of all four reappear and combine. The ending of 'Lurga Lom', in which Lusca takes on the prophesied heroic role of Lurga Lom, in response to the smith's repeated question 'Have you come?' seems to link it to *Potter Thompson*, and to Garner's wider speculations in his books about the role of the hero. Lusca accepts his heroic role and

Potter Thompson refuses his, but they are both affirmative actions.

Potter Thompson, an exploration of the myth of the sleeping hero, 'the prime myth of Britain',[1] was written, according to Garner and Gordon Crosse's programme note, 'to discover why the Hero must always remain asleep'. In it, Garner could remake the bland boy and girl of *The Weirdstone of Brisingamen* and *The Moon of Gomrath* in the image of Gwyn and Alison, Tom and Jan. The Boy and the Girl are the personification of Potter Thompson's pain; on a previous Lughnasa ('Bilberry Night', 'Lunacy Day') he lost his love, and his whole life since has been consumed by regret. While the other villagers revel, the embittered Thompson sits alone on the Hill, knitting. He falls into the Hill (the Edge), pursued by elementals, and 'he undergoes a mystical ordeal of initiation'.[2] He is guided by a strand of wool, like Mary's silk in *The Stone Book*. He comes to the Sleeping Hero, whom he refuses to wake. To wake the Hero would be to deny the promise of the future. The consequence of his waking would be

> '*My head no more*
> *Rampicked by the stars,*
> *No more agait with dreams.*'

His recognition of the importance of the future also relegates the past to its proper perspective, and the Boy and the Girl are freed from its chains:

> '*He takes her by the lily-white hand,*
> *Leads her across the water,*
> *Gives her a kiss and says good-bye;*
> *She is the fairest daughter.*'

Potter Thompson is a complex work (as Hugo Cole wrote in *The Listener*, 'though the plot's simple, the underlying psychology and the use of symbolism are not'),[3] as important to Garner's later development as *Holly from the Bongs* had been to his earlier. It was filmed and transmitted by the BBC in

1975, and was performed at London and Aldeburgh in the same year.

The structure of the four elements and four stages of initiation (parallels with 'primitive' initiation ceremonies are emphasised by the use of bullroarers by the elementals), leading to a fifth, transcendent experience, is well worked out, if somewhat rigid, and many of the thematic and linguistic concerns of the *Stone Book* quartet anticipated. 'The Hill is made from the elements of his craft: earth, water, air and fire. The Elementals who beset him reflect the true image of his soul, and the journey through the Hill is a quest for that soul. But to Thompson it is a headlong flight from the Boy and the Girl of his youth and their crippled love.'[4] Thompson's most affecting solo is a hymn to his craft:

> *'What's clay? You don't know what clay is?*
> *Clay is mother rock*
> *Gathered in a yard of frost.*
> *Mix it with slurry, grog and flint,*
> *And slat it on the wheel.*
> *That's clay for a pot.'*

Elements of Celtic folklore ('My shoe pinches in a place you do not know'; the yarrow love chants) and British nursery rhyme ('Here comes a lusty wooer'), playground chants (the 'yan, tan, tethera, methera' counting formula) and dialect speech ('I'm all collywesson:/My head's going round like cocks and hens') permeate the text; it is soaked in tradition. It is the most overtly mystical of Garner's works, and the first in which a possible happy solution is glimpsed to the landscape of ruptured innocence and betrayed dreams which dominates the first five novels.

The final answer in Potter Thompson's litany identifies the main theme; it is a familiar one:

> *'What moves Earth?*
> *Water.*
> *What moves Water?*

Air.
What moves Air?
Flame.
What moves Flame?
Time.'

Like *Red Shift, Potter Thompson* is fundamentally concerned with time and our perception of it. Potter Thompson is
taken out of time, in order to enable him to come to terms with
the past. At the end 'The magic fades, and we return to the
reality of present time, time-now, the only time in which a
mortal man can live'.[5] As he progresses through the Hill,
voices urge him to 'Remember Time'; Garner writes in his
preface to the script of the TV version, ' "Remember" is
emotionally the antonym of "dismember".'

In 'A Librettist Speaks' Garner writes that it took him
seventeen years to be able to write *Potter Thompson*:

> 'By the time of the fifth novel I knew that I had reached a
> point where the words were picked clean. I was at the
> bone. To have gone further would have been to snap
> syntax and to be in danger of writing a blank page. The
> next words would have to be inflected: they needed to be
> sung.'

The memory of that singing lies behind the rhythms of the
Stone Book quartet.

7

In his *East Cheshire*, written between the dates of *The Stone Book* and *Granny Reardun*, J. P. Earwaker tells us that

> 'HOUGH, or, as it is now more commonly called, "The Hough", is an extensive district which stretches on the east side of the parish, from the village of Wilmslow to the foot of Alderley Edge; and is bounded on the west side by Fulshaw and Chorley. It contains very little of any interest.'

If he but knew. The Hough contained 'all the stories of the world and the flowers of the flood', and it contained the possibility for Alan Garner to come to terms with the anger which had powered his writing and driven him to destroy Tom, Gwyn and Roland.

The *Stone Book* quartet is an act of acceptance. *Red Shift* presented the reader with a maelstrom, an ordered chaos. It was strong, but it reached no resolution, and even after the climax the story petered on in Tom's coded letter printed on the book's endpapers. It ends in disharmony, in a disjointed, lifeless graffito expressing loss, alienation, distress. The quartet picks up the threads and weaves them into a picture of harmony.

The form and style of *Red Shift* were too boldly original for many critics, and it was widely speculated that Garner's undoubted talent was played out. However, if it was possible in 1974 for Justin Wintle to suggest, tentatively, that 'somewhere between Garner's professed admiration for William Golding (whose originality is too idiosyncratic for borrowing) and his own self-absorption, a major talent is energetically destroying itself', it would not be so now, after the publication of the *Stone Book* quartet. The key word in my quotation from Wintle is 'self-absorption': it was possible to feel that the self-analysis and introspection which had yielded the insights into himself and his working methods which Garner revealed in interviews and the insight into human nature which he revealed in his books had nevertheless served to cut him off from the mainstream of life; that his vision was too refined, too intense, too rarefied. In *The Stone Book* and its three successors we discern for the first time that perfect equilibrium between public and private concerns which is the hallmark of mature art. At last the barriers which Garner had so assiduously placed between his art and his readers, barriers linguistic, academic and formal, are down.

In essence the quartet is a further expression of Garner's obsessive need to give time a meaning through the examination of historical cycles, but he has here managed to give expression to a series of highly complex ideas, and life to a number of equally complex characters, in a form so simple as to be available to almost anyone who can read. It is a reaffirmation of his ability to reach children as his first audience; it is his most completely adult statement. The books are simple, slow, uncomplicated, yet their meditative quality is not a dragging, deadening influence for it is channelled through action, and through exuberance.

The quartet is, in a sense, historical fiction, but its form and purposes are other than those of conventional historical fiction. Each of the books is set precisely, the first in 1864, the last in 1941, the others at significant points in the intervening seventy-seven years (1886 and 1916), but they are only

127

perceived as historical from the outside. The tales are felt from within. The perspective which would be gained by stepping outside the child's point of view is achieved instead by analogy and inference from the other three texts. Each of the books can stand alone, but they are best read together, as one work, their narratives understood as part of a web of events, drawing nourishment from and influencing both past and future. Once again, as in *Red Shift* it would have been fatal to let the narrative voice intrude, to assert within the text that the events related are past and done with. The four books are equally present with each other, and equally present with us, the reader.

The style employed is leisured, laconic, yet pregnant with significance, each word holding in its shadow a wider meaning. The stark, staccato effects of *Red Shift* are replaced by full, rounded rhythms, the rhythms not of standard English but of Cheshire speech, perfectly caught. Garner shows great skill both in this (best demonstrated by either reading the books aloud or listening to Garner do so on the records he made of the quartet) and in his use of dialect forms and words. Where these are unfamiliar, and they usually are, their meaning is always plain from their context, without any straining after effect or needless explanation. Words such as 'thrutch', 'raunge', 'pobs' or 'swedgel', meaningless in themselves, seem perfectly natural in context. When Joseph, charmed out of his ungenerous mood by Uncle Charlie's antics, calls him a 'lommering, gawming, kay-pawed gowf' we may not recognise any of the words but their sense is clear, as are the emotions which underly it. Although there is, as Aidan Chambers pointed out in 'Letter from England: A Matter of Balance', a greater proportion of narrative to dialogue in *The Stone Book* than in its immediate predecessors (even the short radio plays Garner fashioned from the books retain a substantial narrative presence), dialogue is still important to Gärner, and his skill in presenting and establishing easily identifiable but not eccentric speech patterns for each character is unerring.

The basis of Alan Garner's work, as with William Mayne, the other major English writer working exclusively in children's books, is an awareness of the symbolic value of language, and this is represented in Garner by the tension between the 'North-West Mercian' language of his heritage and the standard English and classicism of his education, which led to the forsaken 'Ciceronian periods'[1] of his early work. This linguistic symbolism operates on a crude level even in *The Weirdstone of Brisingamen*, in which Gowther speaks cod Cheshire and the evil Morrigan speaks Latin. And in *The Owl Service* it is no accident that the most bitter of Gwyn's taunts of his mother is his observation to her that 'It's uncouth to omit the auxiliary verb'.

The linguistic skirmish is the visible proof of a larger battle, between birthright and education, between lower and middle class, between emotion and logic, instinct and reason; a battle which is won by amalgamation and resolution rather than by outright victory. For in the *Stone Book* quartet Garner has grafted the language of his childhood onto his adult stock, not reverted to it. In 'A View from the Steeple', her admirable review of the quartet, Margaret Meek writes: 'Garner links the continuity of the oral tradition with the modulations of a classical style of great clarity. This counterpoint produces the reverberation of meanings.'

In his fascinating 1978 interview with Aidan Chambers, talking about his attitude to language and his use of dialect, Garner regrets his earlier attempts to reproduce dialect, presumably meaning in the character of Gowther Mossock. Where Gowther's dialect seems wooden and stilted, and on occasions unwarrantably intrusive, the dialect in the *Stone Book* quartet is not only organic to the text but is the perfect vehicle for what Garner has to say. The single quality which most distinguishes the books is the specificity of their imagery, their rooting in a physical world of ploughs, looms, hammers and forges; even the most metaphysical passages are expressed in terms of clock or weathervane. Garner links this quality of his texts with the language he chose to use, the language of a people for whom life is relentlessly physical: 'I have not expressed myself in a direct and concrete way in order to write for a child – I have used this language, which is concrete and direct.' He sums up the three-dimensional, touchable nature of the images through the metaphor of taste: 'I chose a lot of words because I wanted them to taste as I remembered their taste from childhood.'

In this context Ted Hughes' comments on dialect in his *London Magazine* interview with Egbert Faas seem *à propos*. He said:

> 'I grew up in West Yorkshire. They have a very distinctive dialect there. Whatever other speech you grow into, presumably your dialect stays alive in a sort of inner freedom, a separate little self. It makes some things more difficult . . . since it's your childhood self there inside the dialect and that is possibly your real self or the core of it. Some things it makes easier. Without it, I doubt if I would ever have written verse. And in the case of the West Yorkshire dialect, of course, it connects you directly and in your most intimate self to middle English poetry.'

It is this 'inner freedom' over which Garner has in the *Stone Book* quartet regained control. The point about middle English verse is also an important one: the quartet contains numerous nods in the direction of the Gawain poet, and some direct reference. Mary's father's statement in *The Stone Book* that 'I'm the governor of this gang', echoing the Green Knight's challenge in *Sir Gawain and the Green Knight* (' "Wher is", he sayd, /"þe governour of þis gyng?" '), marks an important moment in Garner's artistic development, his discovery, or admission, or assertion that his work forms part of a tradition, and that one of the things he is trying to do is to re-establish for the twentieth-century reader a direct line back to non-Chaucerian middle English, just as MacDiarmid did to the middle Scots poets Dunbar, Henryson and Douglas.

In *Red Shift* Garner was exploring the same linguistic territory as in the *Stone Book* quartet, but the crucial difference is that in the quartet the dialect is in the narrative as well as in the dialogue. The effect is quite different. In *Red Shift* the Cheshire dialogue was often an alienating device, reminding us of Tom's separation from his parents' world, of John Fowler's consciousness of intellectual superiority and emotional inferiority, of the Roman soldiers' inadequate efforts to 'go tribal' convincingly. The quartet, on the other hand, depicts characters who are integrated with their background, in the context of their native culture. Even the feckless Robert in *The Aimer Gate* has his place.

In his 1978 lecture 'The Fine Anger', from which the title of this book is taken, Garner wrote that

'Dialect vocabulary may be used to enrich a text, but it should be used sparingly, and with the greatest precision, otherwise the balance is tipped through the absurd to the obscure. The art is to create the illusion of demotic rather than to record it.'

He recognised, as he had not realised when creating Gowther Mossock, but had in writing *The Owl Service*, that 'The quality . . . is in the cadence'. The extent to which in the *Stone Book* quartet Garner has given the appearance rather than the reality, while persuading the reader that it is the reality, can most easily be seen by the scene in the radio version of *Granny Reardun* in which, for a specific dramatic purpose, the men in the forge, talking behind or beneath the narrator, thicken their dialect till it is almost impassable. 'The dialect switches to a level used only by men when they are at ease in a community of work. The exchanges are like pass-words, ritualistic, shutting out strangers.':

> 'SMITH: Now then, Damper! Come in! Sit thee down. Take thi bacca. Well, Damper, where hast tha bin this journey?
>
> DAMPER: Oh, up atop o' down yonder, miles-endy-ways, tha knows, at Bog o' Mirollies, where cats kittlen magpies.
>
> SMITH: Come thi ways within air o' th' fire, and get some warmship. (TO HIS MEN) We mun weind a bit, lads! Art agate o' gooing, Damper?'

Dialect as broad as this in the books would have seemed quaint and patronising, and in the *Stone Book* quartet Garner is neither of these things. The language is vivid, specific, expressive, direct, but beyond all these things it is purposeful: it is not there for decoration. It is relaxed, but the opposite of lazy. Every possible corner is cut, and the result communicates almost below the level of conscious understanding, because it is the emotional logic of a situation which is expressed, while the situation itself is taken for granted.

The four books centre round the theme of craftsmanship, of the need for each man for his own special 'craft and masterness', and this theme is explored through four vignettes of a single Cheshire family, each book conforming to the unities of time, place and action.

The family is Garner's own; the source material 'anecdotes and oral traditions'.[2] Robert the stonemason in *The Stone Book*, 'a lover of music, a ringer and a singer',[3] is Garner's great-great-grandfather; Mary is his daughter; Joseph the blacksmith is Garner's grandfather, Mary's illegitimate son. These facts are important in that they indicate how far Garner, whose feeling that his education had equipped him to appreciate his culture only by stripping him of it burns in the characters of Gwyn and Tom, has been able to both overcome and use this alienation in portraying and understanding his background. They are not otherwise the critic's concern, just as the real, physical existence of the stone book, the swage block, the cottage, church and chapel, while necessary and important to the writing of the books is of only technical interest when one is considering their literary representations. The real objects and settings of the *Stone Book* quartet are exquisitely realised in Michael Foreman's accompanying etchings, which at their best share in the deep mystery of the texts.

The first of the books, *The Stone Book,* concerns Robert the stonemason and his daughter Mary, and uses stone as a symbol of truth and stability in a rapidly changing world. The new houses, the new school and the new vicarage brought by the railway are linked with their surroundings by the material of which they are built. The central character, Mary, is the only female of note in the quartet: the world examined is a man's world, into which she is only admitted on sufferance, because she has no brother to whom the wonders which her father reveals to her can be shown. She is a surrogate boy, whose fervent hope as she climbs the steeple of St Philip's to bring her father his lunch is that the next child will be a real boy.

The two balanced climaxes of the book, Mary's exhilarating ride on the weathercock and her discovery of the mysterious cave paintings, are finely done, echoing and confirming the texture of the rest of the book rather than providing the sole reason for its existence. The main drift of the argument throughout is that nature and experience are better teachers than books: 'When you cut stone, you see more than the parson does, Church or Chapel.' The proof of Darwin's theories lies deep in the ground, where the parson never ventures, and you can see 'the sea in a hill', just as Colin and Susan notice in the same mines in *The Weirdstone of*

Brisingamen that 'The yellow walls were streaked with browns, blacks, reds, blues and greens – veins of minerals that traced the turn of wind and wave upon a shore twenty million years ago'. Lack of education, however, is nearly as dangerous. Robert's disdain of received opinion, from church or school, has made him 'all povertiness and discontent'.[4] The secret paintings which form the family's link with the past are threatened by the mine-workings; education is the future.

Mary's two visionary experiences are both matched by Robert in *The Aimer Gate*, but while Mary draws from hers a redemptive vision, Robert is only confused and unsettled by his. Robert's climbing of the Chapel steeple, and his discovery of his great-grandfather's mason's mark and their mutual name engraved in the capstone, are experiences as fully mysterious, as potent with meaning, as Mary's, but Robert's inability to interpret the messages of the past or to understand or share his father's delight in the intricacies of the clock's escapement, reflects the book's general mood of waste and failure against the background of the First World War.

In Robert's secret room, as in the Tough Tom clay of Mary's cave, 'the soft floor was covered with footprints, shoes and clogs and boots of every size, covered and filled with droppings, as though all the children from the village and the Moss and the Hough played here. But Robert was every one.' In that one moment he accepts the past, and it accepts him, but the moment is fleeting. Soon he is 'wearing the steeple all the way to the earth, a stone dunce's cap'. When Mary puts her hand to the outline on the cave wall, and makes the connection between 'Fingers and thumb and palm, and a bull and Father's mark in the darkness under the ground', her footprints join those of innumerable forebears, 'no fresher than theirs'. Her lesson is learned permanently, and she has no further need to ask for a book like Annie Leah's and Lizzie Allman's, as the images of the pressed flowers, Old William's silk, the stilled flux in the hill, and the implied refutation of the clergy and book learning, merge into the single powerful symbol of the stone book, which 'showed two fronds of a plant, like the silk in skeins, like the silk on the water under the hill'. Both the first Robert and Joseph greet their children with the same words after their experiences: 'That's put a quietness on you.'

Mary's discovery of the bull has an interesting origin, in the opening lines of a sequel to *Elidor* which were set as a competition to be continued by members of the Puffin Club in 1967. The story is essentially that of 'Feel Free', which was already written by this time:

' "Twenty thousand years ago," said the guide, "pre-historic man used these caves for the practice of his hunting magic. Here in the dark, far underground, he painted these wild boar and antelope on the rock walls, in the hope that this would bring him luck in the chase. That artist pressed his hand, wet with paint, against the cave wall. And now, if you will come this way . . ."
Roland held back, fascinated by the dull brown paint of the hand on the cave. The hand was no bigger than his own, but it was twenty thousand years dead. He set his palm and fingers on the brown. They fitted exactly. But instead of the damp rock, he felt a pressure against his hand, warm, fleshed, and alive as his own.'

When Mary touches the hand 'The rock was cold, but for a moment it had almost felt warm'. The bull has other antecedents, too. It is Theseus' minotaur, and Mary's silk is Ariadne's thread, and it is the magically invoked animals of Altamira and Lascaux. Robert's choice of the rune *tir* as his mason's mark is also significant for *tir* is the name of an old Persian star-sign, 'Arrow', and also the Danish for 'bull'. The sound Robert's hammer makes, 'tac', is another name for the same rune.

The Stone Book was not originally envisaged as part of a sequence, and it is the only one of the four books to make overt connections with magical or religious practices: Daedalus' maze, and beyond it the Troy Town mazes of midsummer games; the initiation ceremonies of Australian aboriginal tribes, in which the initiate is shown a painted symbol called a *churinga,* which is both himself and 'the secret body of the immanent and transcendent ancestor'.[5]

Robert seems at times almost a magus or psychopomp, though he is also always a real man. His making of the stone book is almost described in terms of miracle, certainly when compared, as it has to be, with Joseph's manufacture of the sledge in *Tom Fobble's Day.* Garner's observation that 'He had to take the picture from his eye to his hand before it left him' captures the quality of inspiration, but the ease with which inspiration becomes a 'prayer book bound in blue-black calf skin, tooled, stitched and decorated' may be felt to deny craftsmanship its due.

The stone book is, nevertheless, a wonderful image, unifying the book's spiritual and social concerns. The story's symmetry and grace mark it as an outstanding achievement. The relationships between Mary and her father and Robert and William are drawn with delicacy and clarity, and Mary's ascent and descent realised with great precision.

Like *The Stone Book, Granny Reardun,* the third of the books to be published though the second in chronological sequence, seems to some extent apart from its fellows. It is the only one of the books in which the child character experiences no revelation comparable to William's realisation that he is 'not alone' on his sledge, and Mary and young Robert's experiences in their under- and over-ground caves. Joseph's revelation is of his path to individuality. *Granny Reardun* is also the only book in which the description of Robert making the stone book is not deliberately echoed. *The Stone Book*'s 'turning, tapping, knapping, shaping, twisting, rubbing and making' becomes in *Tom Fobble's Day* 'turning, twisting, tapping, shaping, dabbing and making' and in *The Aimer*

Gate, with a significant change in the final word, 'cutting and snapping, heating, sledging, twisting and breaking', but in *Granny Reardun* the formula makes only an attenuated appearance in 'tapping, drawing'.

The central character in *Granny Reardun*, Joseph, plays a crucial role in both *The Aimer Gate* and *Tom Fobble's Day*, appearing as boy, father and grandfather. In a sense the quartet can be seen as Joseph's story in much the same way as W. J. Gruffyd saw the Four Branches of the Mabinogi as relating the birth, youthful exploits, maturity/imprisonment (Joseph is shackled by the demands of the war) and death of Pryderi.

Joseph is Mary's illegitimate child, and the theme of illegitimacy, revisited for the first time since *The Owl Service*, is handled with subtlety and compassion, and forms a powerful undercurrent to the main story, even though many of its readers may not at once understand why Joseph is a 'granny reardun', or why that should count against him. As in *The Stone Book* self-discovery is paralleled by images of needless destruction and inhumanity; Joseph's realisation that he wants to be a smith, because 'a smith's aback of everything' unfolds in counterpoint to the story of the Allmans' eviction from their home so that its stone may be used to build a kitchen garden. The story is, as so many of Garner's have been, of the need of each generation to escape the shadow of the last. Joseph cannot be a mason: he has no feel for it, and his grandfather 'was everywhere, all over . . . But I got aback of him.'

Despite a considerable charm, and a number of vivid and memorable moments ('the church was the print of chisels in the sky') *Granny Reardun* is in many ways the least satisfying of the four. It lacks the religious sense of *The Stone Book*, the violent hopelessness of *The Aimer Gate*, the triumphant coherence of *Tom Fobble's Day*. It is the most inward-looking, the most self-contained of the four.

The Aimer Gate, like *Tom Fobble's Day*, looks outward to war. It is possibly the most perfect book of the four, and its perfection can be seen by comparing it briefly with the first section of John Fowles' *Daniel Martin*, 'The Harvest'. Fowles is the only other English novelist of Garner's generation of comparable stature, and his concerns in *Daniel Martin* are close to Garner's in the quartet: 'The Harvest' is a statement of belonging to the English countryside and the rhythms of country life, and, like *The Aimer Gate*, centres round a wartime harvest and the slaughter of the rabbits as the last hay is cut. Fowles' lush descriptions cannot equal Garner's savage reticence: Uncle Charlie's pain is all the more striking for being concealed, and makes Daniel Martin's fear of death seem histrionic; Garner's spareness makes Fowles' lyricism seem spurious. The portentousness of 'see him scythe, dwarf the distort handle and the blade, the swaling drive and unstopping rhythm, pure and princely force of craft' seems hollow beside Garner's picture of the reapers 'like a big clock, back and to, back and to, against the hill', an image which both forms a link between the book's exterior and interior settings and echoes the description of the sea in *The Stone Book* and of the movement of Damper Latham's head and shoulders as he sings in *Granny Reardun*.

The Aimer Gate (Wright's *English Dialect Dictionary* has 'a more direct road' for 'aimer gate'; the use of the phrase as a metaphor for death seems to be Garner's own) was originally to be called *Litherman's Load*, defined by Darlington, whose *The Folk-Speech of South Cheshire* is an important linguistic source for the quartet, as 'a lazy man's load; a load piled up to save the trouble of a double journey'. The change of title shifts the emphasis from Robert to Uncle Charlie, the sniper. Garner's notes for the book include, amid lists of slang place-names on the Western Front, the curt observation 'Uncle Charlie a joking loner. Trickster.' Charlie is an outsider, marked for death. It is the waste of his generation on the battlefields of France that is reflected in Robert's inability to settle to a craft.

The only crafts or skills in use in *The Aimer Gate* are Joseph's half-brother Uncle Charlie's parallel ones of scything and soldiering, and the narrative is grimly punctuated by the senile militarism of legless Faddock Allman, the lively 'Young Herbert' of *Granny Reardun*, reduced by the Boer War to life in a makeshift cart, breaking up the stones from his family's old house for use as road flints. Joseph's skills as 'the only best smith from Chorley to Mottram' are disregarded, devoted to the menial task of supplying horseshoes for the war effort; there is nothing that Robert has the 'flavour' of: Joseph tells him 'I don't know what there is for you to get aback of, youth'.

There is nothing; not, that is, until Uncle Charlie tells him 'Get aback of me' as he exercises his skill and craft. He is blowing the heads off rabbits with ruthless precision as they flee from their last refuge, 'the last standing corn', to the ironic, hollow sound of the 'Who-whoop! Wo-whoop! Wo-o-o-o! Who-Whoop! Wo-whoop! Wo-o-o-o!' which rings through the (chronologically) first three books. However, Robert's vague desire to go for a soldier has already been scorned by Charlie, whose intimations of mortality ('I might just go the aimer gate this time') are confirmed in *Tom Fobble's Day*. His name is one of those on the War Memorial, as is Ozzie Leah's. What eventually does happen to Robert is unclear, but his absence from *Tom Fobble's Day* is an ominous one. When Uncle Charlie tells him that 'You want craft and masterness in you' he is using the word want to mean lack as well as need or desire. Robert will follow neither his great-grandfather Robert nor his father Joseph, though he shares many of Joseph's qualities, including his reaction to distress. When the Allmans are evicted in *Granny Reardun*, and Robert the stonemason and Damper start to sing,[6] Joseph cannot play his cornet: 'His neck hurt for thought of the Allmans.' When Robert tries to sing 'Can You Wash a

Soldier's Shirt?' to the accompaniment of Joseph's cornet, Charlie's rifle and Faddock Allman's senile shouts of 'Retreat! Forward! Charge!' he 'couldn't sing. His neck hurt.'

The reasons for Joseph's fury at Faddock's presence are never articulated, and need not be extrapolated by the reader. It is the pitch of the emotions which is important, not their cause. There could be any number of reasons for Joseph's antipathy to Faddock. The strongest is one of class: Joseph is a skilled man, whose skills are being subverted by war, a craftsman proud of being a Houghite; Faddock is a labourer, an unskilled Mossaggot. Joseph is master in his own home, and has not been asked if Faddock can be fed. What is more, Faddock is a reminder of Joseph's unfitness for active service (he has hammer toes; he is the lame smith). As far as the book is concerned, Faddock is important as an image of war's destructive wastefulness.

The Aimer Gate is essentially an unhappy book, but even here the disturbing image of the dying rabbits, whose 'screaming pierced all noise' resolves into a picture of calm and harmony, as the symbolism of the clock, which has already incorporated the traditional rhythms of the harvest, forms a bridge between the instruments of creation and destruction: 'Father and Uncle Charlie played the great tune of the Hough, E Flat cornet and rifle, on either side of the fire, and the day swung in the chapel clock, escapement to the sun.'

Tom Fobble's Day is the opposite side of the coin. Whereas in *The Aimer Gate* the war inspires a sense of aimless disillusionment, in *Tom Fobble's Day* the sledge, symbolic of all the crafts which have gone towards its making, symbolic too of the lessons written in the stone book, with the making of which Joseph's manufacture of the sledge is a conscious parallel, rides freely and easily over the jagged shrapnel which has 'brogged the snow' (just as the grass is 'brogged by old cow muck' in *Granny Reardun*). The searchlights and air raids add a sense of excitement, not danger, and William's pretence that he is a Spitfire gives him his most satisfying and total victory over Stewart Allman.

Tom Fobble's Day brings the sequence up to 1941, and offers a final synthesis of the images of sledge (and pram), loom, forge, stone and field which pervade the earlier three books (two of which were, of course, actually written and published after *Tom Fobble's Day*). The sledge which Joseph makes his grandson William from the remnants of loom and forge, the key which was his first prentice piece as a smith and the discovery of the first Robert's Macclesfield Dandy pipe, dropped in *The Stone Book*, like a fossil in the potato hogg, provide the bullied and nervous boy with a link with his past and family so concrete that he no longer fears sledging; he is part of the landscape. 'There was a line, and he could feel it. It was a line through hand and eye, block, forge and loom to the hill. He owned them all: and they owned him.'[7] He negotiates the dangerous hump which is all that is left of the Allmans' cottage with no difficulty at all.

Like *The Stone Book*, *Tom Fobble's Day* has long origins: Garner's note of the Tom Fobble's Day custom from George Ewart Evans' *Ask the Fellows Who Cut the Hay* is dated 11 May 1966. As in the other books, it is the immediacy with which Garner evokes feelings, experiences, places, characters which is so impressive: the picture of Joseph is particularly fine, affectionate but never sentimental. *Tom Fobble's Day* is not without its darker undertones, but it moves towards strength and joy.

There is in the book, as throughout the quartet, a constant sense of something more, something greater, behind the events described, an alchemical transmutation of the dross of everyday into the gold of *every day*. It is in his control over this sense of incipient revelation, his ability not to impose but to perceive and to reveal pattern and meaning in his characters' lives, that Garner transcends in the quartet the traditional family saga.

A finely written northern working-class example of this genre published in 1976, the year before *Tom Fobble's Day*, David Storey's *Saville*, contains a parallel wartime sledging incident, and a comparison of the two treatments is illuminating. Colin's father's building of the sledge in *Saville* is reported in the past tense ('When Colin came home from school at lunch-time a sledge was standing half-completed . . . When he came home at tea-time the sledge was finished'); the building components that are detailed are lifeless bits of metal, wood and rope. In *Tom Fobble's Day* the action of making, not the objects made, is the focus of attention, and the materials are quickened by our sense of their past.

Storey's approach is one of careful decription of the minutiae of life, supplemented by occasionally ponderous Lawrentian analysis of emotion; Garner's is the reliving of essential moments, and the embodiment of emotion in the silences between his characters' speeches. Storey works from outside, Garner from within. Without disrespect to David Storey or to *Saville*, a writer and a book I admire, it seems to me to be clear that Garner's achievement is both the more difficult and the more substantial. In the sledging episodes, for instance, Storey evokes the fun and the rivalry of the occasion, but can only hint at the mystery which Garner faces full on. To compare the closing pages of *Tom Fobble's Day* with Storey's final sledging paragraph is to see how magically Garner has, without distortion, transformed the meaning of what he describes. Storey writes:

> 'Often he was the last on the slope, waiting for the others to grow tired and leave, pulling their sledges slowly up to the gate, their voices fading down the road. Sometimes, when he had come down the track, he lay on the sledge, his cheek on the snow that had frozen to the wood, his breath rising in a thin mist past his face, the hill silent, glowing faintly, the odd calls, the barking of a dog and the shutting of doors coming from the houses

beyond. A moon had risen on the second night: it shone as a bright disc, the track like a strip of metal running between the smooth mounds on either side. Towards the town, as the night settled, there was the faint probing of searchlights, moving like stiff fingers, slowly waving to and fro.'

Of course, Storey is not trying here, or elsewhere in *Saville*, to convey the sort of mystical epiphanies recorded by Garner, but he is trying to portray a similar culture, and using a child and a child's experiences as the instrument of understanding. It seems to me that Garner's heightened awareness of the immediate moment gives the reader a truer perspective than Storey's traditional novelist's stance of historical objectivity. In Storey we may visualise the setting; in Garner we smell, taste, feel it.

There is nothing in *Saville*, indeed there is nothing else in Garner to match the exhilaration of the scene when William runs from the dead Joseph's house with the horseshoes he has 'Tom Fobbled' from the chimney, where they were placed as a 'mystery' and a blessing like the thunderstone in Thomas and Margery's hearth:

'The line did hold. Through hand and eye, block, forge and loom to the hill and all that he owned, he sledged sledged sledged for the black and glittering night and the sky flying on fire and the expectation of snow.'

The *Stone Book* quartet (Garner originally intended the books to bear the overall title *Bollin Fee*, the old name of the area in which they are set, and in some interviews refers to them as such) is difficult to criticise. Even to quote from the books is hard, because so much of the meaning of each fragment depends on its place in the whole. The books have the density of poetry but the flow of prose; they rely heavily on poetic techniques, assonance, alliteration, half-rhyme, rhythm, for their effect. They are Garner's most successful attempt yet to convey in words 'the sacramental dimensions of human existence', which is how he defined his central concern in his 1975 lecture 'Moving Language'. The books are an attempt to write the unwritable, say the unsayable, and they have an inner privacy of which any critical words, however commendatory, seem a violation.

It is hard to resist the idea that the quartet is the expression of something highly personal to Garner, of his discovery of a means of rejoining his ancestors by putting his learned skills at the service of theirs. Behind the four published books is a fifth, implied book, about the craft of the writer. Garner says:

> 'There is one moment of hubris which I allow myself, and that is seeing the international copyright sign . . . then my name and the date, and then I know I've written that book. It lasts for a second, possibly two, and then I do feel, with my father and my grandfather, and my great-grandfather.'[8]

For Garner the quartet is his 'major work',[9] and as a critic I do not feel disposed to argue. The gift for characterisation, the ear for dialogue, the feeling for landscape, the ability to seize upon the transcendent moment and communicate its meaning without analysis, the sustaining sense of history and the extraordinary grasp of human experiences in relation to one another rather than in a vacuum, a sense not merely of the individual thread but also of its place in the web, are at last in the quartet put to the service of a unifying vision of grace, or at least the possibility of it.

Until the *Stone Book* quartet Garner's is essentially a bleak vision of a world blighted by materialism, where 'things' are 'more than thoughts':[10] his themes are loneliness, isolation, jealousy, failure, the destructive power of possessive love, 'betrayal and the loss of innocence'.[11] The stabs of humour are either black, as in his verses 'R.I.P.' and 'Carol', or bitter, as in

Gwyn's cracks in *The Owl Service* or Tom's in *Red Shift*. In the quartet, without any sentimentalisation, we feel loving-kindness balanced against cruelty, companionship against isolation, life against death. The image of Joseph and Charlie playing 'Can you wash a soldier's shirt?' with cornet and rifle is not simply a disturbing one, it is also comic, and, despite the elegaic mood, harmonious.

Though the quartet is firmly placed in an historical as well as a geographical context, and though the family on whom it is based is a real one, in one sense it is as invented as anything Garner has written. His statement, about *The Stone Book*, that 'it had to be Mary the girl because Mary was her name and she was a girl'[12] is disingenuous: he has not, as this suggests, abdicated artistic responsibility; rather, he uses the oral and written history of his family as the exact equivalent of the myths and historical research on which he drew in his previous books. It is Garner who climbed the steeple, not Mary;[13] the geological insights and their spiritual significance relate to his own extraordinary childhood experiences.[14] The incidents described in the books are not real in the sense that the Barthomley massacre was real; they are related not to slavishly follow reality but to reveal inner truth. The books are 'the emotional history of one rural family';[15] the incidents selected or invented are those which can bear the full symbolic weight of the whole, rather than those which could be held to be representative or typical. It is the delicacy of their expression which makes them deserve our attention, not their veracity: as Brian Alderson wrote when only two of the books were published, they 'seem to lie beyond any making'.[16]

8

Garner's work since the *Stone Book* quartet: *The Lad of the Gad*, the *Fairytales of Gold, Lamaload, To Kill a King*, gives little indication of the direction of his next move. It may be that another of his minor works, his poem *The Breadhorse*, published in 1975, is a more helpful pointer.

The Breadhorse is a strange text, centred round a repeated Romany refrain culled from Borrow's *The Bible in Spain*. The blurb describes the cry

> *'Kosko gry! Rommany gry!*
> *Muk man kistur tute knaw.'*

as 'used by the Rommanies to control their excited horses'. It is not, as this suggests, a traditional rhyme or spell, but rather an impromptu of Borrow's when he leapt on to a nervous and dangerous horse; it seems to mean

> *'Good horse! Gypsy horse!*
> *Let me ride you now.'*

As Garner uses it, adding a touch of wild splendour to the rituals of the playground, it seems almost identified with the mystical 'Horseman's Word' by use of which those in the know were reputed to exercise an uncanny mastery over all horses.[1] Borrow suggests such a connection: he uses the words just after asking his servant Antonio 'Are there whisperers in your country?'

Based on the playground game of breadhorses, in which one child must carry the others for a reward of bread (or chocolate), the poem stars Ned, who can't whistle or spit, which is why

> '*I'm always It*
> *For Breadhorses.*'

In both *Red Shift* and *To Kill a King* to call a person 'It' is seen as the ultimate dehumanising act; *The Breadhorse* is the story of Ned's fight back into humanity, through dreams. He has a dream of riding a glorious, archetypal horse, which is the final culmination of the shadow/light imagery I discussed in chapter 5. As he lies on his bed:

> '*My shadow grew bright*
> *And I could feel*
> *That what was dark*
> *Was covered in light*
> *And a yellow mane.*'

He is enabled to share his dream, and carry his friends

> '*On my shadow's light.*'

Although like all Garner's work *The Breadhorse* resists any simplistic statement of its meaning, it seems to have to do with the freedom of the imagination to create and to be secure in creation. Ned is a Roland who comes to terms with his dream; Roland may resemble Findhorn, Ned *is* the horse he rides: 'Red horse or white/Breadhorse or me/We were all the same.' The golden mane, too, suggests further connections: with the stable boy who turns into a horse in *The Princess and the Golden Mane*, but also with Malebron's yellow hair.

The poetic gift Garner revealed in *Holly from the Bongs*, which shapes his prose, gave form to *Potter Thompson* and flashes briefly from *The Breadhorse* is realised again in 'The Island of the Strong Door', a poem written to accompany a series of photographs of megalithic stones by Paul Caponigro.

147

'The Island of the Strong Door', which draws on Celtic myth and legend and quotes the 'Song of Amergin' and Taliesin's wind poem, seems a first attempt at defining a possible future voice. It is a hymn to the numinous essence of the British landscape, to 'the Celtic cycle that lies, a subterranean influence as a deep water troubling, under every tump in this Island, like Merlin complaining under his big rock'.[2]
The Grail castle is described,

> 'In the island of the strong door.
> In the four-cornered castle.
> In the spinning circle.
> In the garth of glass.'

and identified, as in *The Moon of Gomrath*, and, visually, in *Lamaload*, with water held in the land:

> 'A long sound
> In the flint answered the field
> And the wood. Beyond the crest
> Pools cupped water in sarsen,
> Below were stones.'

The first section of the poem seems almost spoken by the stones, the second by the wind, the third by the land, the next three by Garner himself, and in the seventh and last the voices merge. I am by no means sure that I understand what the poem is about, but I feel its power, the controlled pulse of ritual statement.

It is only in the seventh section that meaning becomes really obscured, as if the images were too compressed, too esoteric, or possibly as if Garner has been unable to catch or contain his thought. Certainly the last two lines seem lax and conventional, an anticlimactic dispersal of the tension which the rest of the poem has built up, rather than, as they should be, a coherent insight into the link between 'Flintshard and skull' and 'the exploding blood'.

Whether or not 'The Island of the Strong Door' leads

anywhere, and whether or not its images will be clarified in future work, it is a clear proof of the continuing vitality of Garner's imagination.

'The Island of the Strong Door', though it is clearly directed at an adult audience, is linked no less securely than *The Breadhorse* to the body of Garner's work. The last three lines of section six might be a statement of the predicament of the *Red Shift* protagonists:

> *'Hinged on the sky*
> *It is lonely, it is lonely,*
> *And the miles between.'*

This insistent cross-fertilisation between pieces of writing, the sense of overriding vision, is, as I have already noted, one of the dominating characteristics of Garner's art. It is sometimes difficult to know when to stop enumerating the connections: when Tom compulsively counts the tesserae at Euston Station, should we think of Roland in the stone circle ('You must stay here till you have counted them all') or of the hero of Garner's morbid schoolboy piece 'Mauldeth Road Station', who performs similar futile mathematical feats? The radio play of *The Stone Book* opens with Old William singing 'I'll dye, I'll dye my petticoat red'; Thomas Venables sings the same song in *Red Shift*; Garner collected it from Joshua Birtles, the 'original' of Gowther Mossock, and played the tape of it in the first of his four 1962 radio talks 'Four Hairy Herrings'. The third of these talks, 'Bungnippers, Mooncursers and Strowling-Morts', includes the line, running straight to *Tom Fobble's Day*, 'when I was at school, "brogging" was to spoil a slide'.

Similarly, Campbell's *Popular Tales* are a submerged presence from *The Weirdstone of Brisingamen* to their emergence in *The Lad of the Gad* (Huw's comment to Roger 'You have raven's knowledge?' is from Campbell, for instance; *Tha fios fithich agud*, thou hast raven's knowledge,

149

is 'said to children who are unusually knowing things of which they have no ostensible means of gaining knowledge'); *The Destruction of Da Derga's Hostel*, too, continually resurfaces, from 'The Star of Galgoid' to the title of *To Kill a King*, which is taken from the last line of 'House by Jodrell', adapted from *Da Derga*:

'A night to kill a king is this night.'

Themes: time, place, isolation, alienation, twinning, innocent love betrayed, confrontation with the divine, redemption, recur in the same way. As Garner put it in 'Coming to terms': 'it is the same story every time only in different guises'. Both parts of this statement are true: Garner may rework the same themes but he does not retread the same ground.

Time, 'the moving image of unmoving eternity',[3] is perhaps the most constant theme of all. In Eliade's writings on shamanism and primitive cosmology and the 'acausal connecting principle' of Jungian synchronicity Garner found an intellectual framework which would hold his insights and allow him to develop a fiction in which sequential, causal, 'historical' time is set against and enlarged by a 'mythological' concept of time as elastic, cyclic, recoverable. Time dissolves in the snow in *The Weirdstone of Brisingamen*; the Eve of Gomrath is 'one of the four nights of the year when Time and Forever mingle'; for Alison ' "Yesterday", "today", "tomorrow" – they don't mean anything. I feel they're here at the same time: waiting.' In 'The Edge of the Ceiling' Garner reveals that as a child he played games with time 'as if it were chewing-gum', as Gwyn does when he waits in the dark for Alison: 'I had to. If I had not kept time pliant, it would have set me like the pebble in the rock.'

Myth is the crucible in which Garner's thinking about time has been fired. As Eliade has shown, myth in one of its functions is a means by which man can transcend the historical present and enter the eternal present. Once the connection had been made strongly enough, in *The Owl Service*, a Stone Age axe or a painted hand were sufficient to reactivate it.

Though Garner's use of myth has altered considerably during his career it has always been used to sharpen our perception of emotional, intellectual or spiritual potentials which are either crushed or ignored in a materialistic, vicarious society. He has not been concerned primarily to entertain, though he has been concerned that his books should be entertaining, but to provoke, to stimulate, to extend.

It is true that the mythology in *The Weirdstone of Brisingamen* and *The Moon of Gomrath* is in some ways used simply as a crutch for his inexperience, but this is only part of the truth. He writes in his note to *The Moon of Gomrath* that 'The more I learn, the more I am convinced that there are no original stories. On several occasions I have 'invented' an incident, and then come across it in an obscure fragment of Hebridean lore, orally collected and privately printed a hundred years ago.' Originality, therefore, lies not in invention but in 'the personal colouring of existing themes'. The author is as concerned with transmitting as with creating. Also, we do find in *The Moon of Gomrath* a first tentative marshalling of myth as something more than decoration. Although the evidence to suggest that Morrigu, or any other female Celtic deity, triple or otherwise, was particularly associated with the moon is small, and the idea is thus derived more from Graves than from tradition, the association of moon and blood in Susan's magical powers, and her gradual coming into awareness of those powers, offers a powerful symbol of developing sexuality which while it is never fully worked out is also never overstrained.

Garner turned to myth because of a concern, central to his writing, with the patterning of life, and with the relationship of the present to the past. Gradually, the myth receded, as he found stories which would hold the charge which in the first two books is supplied by the folklore, not the characters. Colin and Susan are separated from home and family, and it is in the tensions of the home that his future interest was to lie. In the conflicting needs of children to both supplant, succeed and escape their parents and to love, imitate and obey them, Garner found stories to match the power of his sources and models. As his career has proceeded he has concentrated more and more on the central pattern, approaching his themes directly rather than obliquely through the mediation of myth. The ingredients of myth have been replaced by the feel of myth, by books which operate in a mythological dimension. Myth and folklore have not been shed, but have been relegated to a deeper level of the books' structure, so that *Red Shift* can be said to contain not only 'Tam Lin' but the whole of *The Guizer*. Be it the Fourth Branch of the Mabinogi in *The Owl Service* or the family lore and research into folk life and folk speech in the *Stone Book* quartet, myth and folklore shape Garner's work, and enable him to distance himself from his material.

In a sense Garner uses mythological elements for the resonances they afford to the reader growing up with the books. With rereading and the passing of time one's appreciation of the books is deepened and sustained by their links with a wider body of literature and lore. When we read in *The Moon of Gomrath* that the sleeping king's sword could 'draw blood from the wind' we do not need to know that this is the phrase used of Culhwch's battle-axe in 'Culhwch and Olwen', but our attention is drawn to the corresponding sharpness of the image when we do learn it. Similarly, it is unimportant to recognise in Atlendor's 'Move not a sinew of thy sinews' the words of Conall from J. F. Campbell's 'Conall', just as we need not notice in Robert's 'time and arithmetic' speech in *The Stone Book* quotations from the seventeenth-century Biblical scholar John Lightfoot. Such touches, indeed, serve their purpose of imparting 'authenticity' to the narrative only when instant recognition of their source is not invited. Our enjoyment of Garner's books is never substantially lessened by ignorance of his sources; his use of myth is neither obscurantist nor escapist.

Why should a writer whose chief concerns are the nature of time and the nature of religious experience come to rest on the children's list? Partly, it seems a reflection of Garner's unwillingness to make any statement before he is ready to do so, before he has reduced (increased?) his ideas to their simplest, their essential form. While the inner world is complex, its truths are simple truths, and whatever the complexities beneath the surface no articulation of inner space can be satisfactory which does not reflect this in a surface simplicity which renders it accessible to all.

Another answer to the question of why an author of such power and originality should have addressed himself, or found his work addressed, to children and adolescents, may be found in his statement to Iain Finlayson that 'I have not yet found satisfactory answers to any of the questions I asked before the age of eighteen and all the questions I have resolved, intellectually, have been questions I have asked after that age. The important questions are asked in childhood and they are never resolved.' It is with these 'important questions', the fundamental mysteries of life which are so often ignored by the adult as insoluble and therefore irrelevant, that he is concerned. The tentative solutions to which he comes about them are reached by prowling the border country of adolescence, finding an equilibrium between the instinctual life of the child and the cerebral life of the adult.

Garner seems to feel that in adulthood we lose touch with our essential nature, that the perceived opposition of the self to the world (the artificial separation of the inner and outer worlds) that is regarded by our society as a sign of maturity is actually a block to our understanding. Children, he told

153

Finlayson, appear to appreciate his work 'with greater perception perhaps because they have not dis-integrated'. Mary's father is not referring simply to the difficulties of physical access to the cave paintings when he tells her that 'We have to go before we're too big to get past the fall, though I reckon, years back, the road was open; if you knew it was there'. So, Garner writes in Aidan Chambers' *The Reluctant Reader*,

> 'I'm a children's writer because Collins decide to put me on their children's list. Yet I do want children to read the books, and especially do I want adolescents to find them. Simply, children make the best audience. Connect with a child and you really connect. Adolescence is the same only more so.'

It seems to me also that Garner's decision to write for children was to some extent a symbolic rejection of the plastic adult world he satirises in 'Feel Free', and which by the act of becoming a writer he refused to join. To his children and adolescents 'the potential universe is open';[4] until *The Stone Book* his adults, with the exception of the slightly quaint Mossocks and of the divine fool Huw, are boorish, weak or uncomprehending. The Elidor Treasures, symbols of the life of the spirit which is denied by the adult world, interfere with that world's totem object, the television, Tom's dreaded 'corpse candles' in *Red Shift*. Colin and Susan's reaction to the vulgarities of the tourists on Alderley Edge is typical: 'This place, where beauty and terror had been as opposite sides of the same coin, was now a playground of noise. Its spirit was dead, or hidden.'

This inability to treat the adult's world as seriously as the child's has now been overcome; he has still to find some way of either freeing his imagination from its narrowing, limiting image of woman as either earth mother or world bitch or, more likely, of channelling that image into a more fruitful perception, a process which has perhaps been set under way in *The Lad of the Gad*. The world of the *Stone Book* quartet is too rich to admit such a stereotype undigested, and it is significant that although the society it depicts is to a certain extent a matriarchal one (Joseph is a 'granny' reardun) women are rigidly excluded from the books. Mary's mother lies down on her bed in *The Stone Book* and says one line in *Granny Reardun*, but Mary is the only female character, and she, as she herself sees, is merely a substitute boy.

It may be that Garner will develop the sense of ironic detachment from this simplistic view of women as, whether nurturing or devouring, essentially passive, instinctual, uncerebral, acted on rather than acting, which will enable him to explore a world in which that stereotype operates with the same perception which he has brought to the masculine world of work and craftsmanship, to the Cheshire landscape and to the problems of time and history. Certainly without it his books lack an important dimension.

Though *Red Shift* gains from this surrendering to the archetype in the coherence and strength of its symbolism it definitely suffers in the depiction of Jan. There is no question of Jan not being a rounded or a convincing character, for she is both, but the mistake she makes when she attempts to rationalise her relationship with Tom, to move from the instinctual to the cerebral, is obscured rather than clarified by being the culmination of a narrative in which cerebration is seen as a purely masculine activity and the spontaneous action on the affections as a purely feminine prerogative. When Margery assaults John Fowler she is not taking on a man's role, she is a lioness defending her cub. The women are not allowed to think.

For Garner, as for Graves, 'man does, woman is'. This is made clear in *The Moon of Gomrath*. After Albanac has explained that the Old Magic, of which the Hunter is the chief representative, is 'woman's magic', Susan asks

' "What does the Hunter do? What's he for?"
"Do? He *is*, Susan: that is enough." '

Nevertheless, Garner's achievement has been large. The *Stone Book* quartet, at least, will last. How his talent will develop is unpredictable. It seems unlikely that he will write any more fantasies, and unlikely, too, that his best future work will be for children. The qualities which have placed him at the head of any list of contemporary children's writers, his sensitive and vital use of myth, his hard-edged economy, his skill with dialogue, his alertness to verbal patterns and strong sense of structure, are skills equally useful to the novelist, the poet, or the dramatist, and need not confine him to the children's lists if he has said all he has to say in that vein. Whatever he says, in whatever mode, will be worth listening to. His themes are large, urgent, passionate, compassionate, his voice distinguished by clarity, compression, precision, depth of feeling and sharpness of thought.

He is concerned with the traversal of boundaries inside the self, with the refinement of consciousness. Through the manipulation of history, of the myths which are man's spiritual history and of the metaphysics of time and space he enlarges our understanding of the human condition, of the relationship of man to man, of man to nature, and of man to god. Essentially, he seeks in his work to reconcile 'the natural forces in the world and the hidden forces in ourselves'.[5] His books are a search for the numinous, for the aspect of the human mind which has been allowed to atrophy in the development of the rational intelligence,[6] through the continual reworking of a few themes within a conceptual framework which stresses at one extreme timelessness, prophecy, transcendent experience and at the other the need to recreate and recapture the past, not out of any feeling of nostalgia but to validate and define the present, and to make possible a rooted, not a rootless future.

Notes

Preface

1 This quotation is from Ronald Bryden's article 'The Man Who Created "The Owl Service"'.

Introduction

1 Garner has frequently mentioned the catalytic effect of his discovery of Golding's work. See for instance Michael Moynihan 'Dark Dreams at Toad Hall'.

2 Alan Garner 'Who, How, Why'.

3 Dennis Hart 'Allen Garner'.

Chapter 1

1 To be found in K. M. Briggs *A Dictionary of British Folk-Tales* B.2, p. 398; the version which serves as a foreword to *The Weirdstone of Brisingamen* is, as Garner took it from an oral source (see Jennifer Farley 'Bardic Ring – Feminine Mystery') as 'authentic' as any, and contains all the main points of the story as told by Thomas Broadhurst, 'Old Daddy', the servant of the Stanleys of Alderley from whom the first printed version (in the *Manchester Mail* in 1805) was taken. See W. E. A. Axon *Cheshire Gleanings* for various versions and analogues of the tale. Two Victorian versifications of the legend can be found in Egerton Leigh *Ballads and Legends of Cheshire*.

2 All quotations from *The Weirdstone of Brisingamen*, unless otherwise stated, are from the revised text of 1963. Quotations from Alan Garner's other works are from the first English edition, unless otherwise stated.

3 Garner's note gives the origins of the spells. For the words of power on Susan's bracelet, see A. E. Waite *The Book of Black Magic*

and of Pacts pp. 95–6.

4 This version of Cuchulain's death is given in T. W. Rolleston's *Myths and Legends of the Celtic Race*, which was one of the series of books about various mythologies published by Harrap which were Garner's first introduction to the world of myth (see *The Hamish Hamilton Book of Goblins* p. 222); their imprint can be traced throughout his work. The other eleven titles are the works by F. M. Davis, M. I. Ebbutt, H. A. Guerber, W. M. Petrovich, and Coomaraswamy and Nivedita listed in the bibliography, and J. L. T. C. Spence's *The Myths of Mexico and Peru, Myths and Legends of the North American Indians, The Myths of Ancient Egypt* and *Myths and Legends of Babylonia and Assyria*. When Garner writes that the twelve volumes were 'published by Harrap between 1915 and 1917' he must be referring to the dates of the reprints purchased by his great-grandfather rather than those of original publication.

5 See W. E. A. Axon *Nixon's Cheshire Prophecies*.

6 For the story of the huldufolk see J. Simpson *Icelandic Folktales and Legends* p. 14.

7 The forms 'Fimbul-winter' and 'Managarm', along with Ymir, Ragnarok, Nidhug, Orgelmir, Maras (described as female trolls), Lios-Alfar, Einheriar, Grimnir, the stag Nurathror (not Durathror; it is given in this form in Auden and Taylor *The Elder Edda* 'The Lady of Grimnir' p. 67) and Gondemar, king of the dwarfs, are to be found in the relevant Harrap volume, H. A. Guerber *Myths of the Norsemen from the Eddas and Sagas*, as is the story of Freya's necklace Brisinga-men, in which mention of Freya's 'falcon garb' may have suggested Durathror's power of flight.

8 See Gruffyd *Math vab Mathonwy* pp. 147–8.

9 See *Beowulf*, ed. A. J. Wyatt lines 1197–9. See also *Widsith* ed. R. W. Chambers pp. 30–1, 33.

10 Alan Garner, note to *The Moon of Gomrath*. Gwyddno Garan(h)ir was a Welsh hero-king, ruler of a submerged kingdom in Welsh folk tradition. Rachel Bromwich translates Garanir as 'Long-shank' (*Trioedd Ynys Prydein* p. 241); I have encountered no evidence to suggest that this was ever the name of a horned god. The second name given, 'Gorlassar', is taken from 'The Death-Song of Uthyr Pendragon' (Skene *The Four Ancient Books of Wales* Book 1 p. 297: 'Am I not he that is called Gorlassar').

11 *The Moon of Gomrath* chapter 9:
'They were all in red: red were their tunics, and red their cloaks; red their eyes, and red their long manes of hair bound back with circlets

of red gold; three red shields on their backs, and three red spears in their hands; three red horses under them, and red was the harness. Red were they all, weapons and clothing and hair, both horses and men.'

The Destruction of Da Derga's Hostel p. 28:

'Three red frocks had they, and three red mantles: three red bucklers they bore, and three red spears were in their hands: three red steeds they bestrode, and three red heads of hair were on them. Red were they all, both body and hair and raiment, both steeds and men.'

Note the comparative richness of Garner's reworking, the sensuous delight in description and rhythm for their own sake.

12 See 'Hanes Taliessin' in Guest *The Mabinogion* vol. 3 p. 373: 'My original country is the region of the summer stars.' Annwm is not, of course, simply the land of the dead.

13 See Graves *The White Goddess* chapter 3.

14 See for instance *An Islamic Book of Constellations*, intro. Emmy Wellesz.

15 Angharad's words in chapter 13 about the horn are taken almost directly from 'The Colloquy with the Ancients', S. H. O'Grady *Silva Gadelica* p. 102.

16 The version in 'Coming to Terms' is slightly misquoted.

17 Garner himself enjoyed a distinguished athletic career as a schoolboy: in 1952 he could run 100 yards in 10.2 seconds and was rated 'the fastest schoolboy sprinter in Great Britain' (*Ulula* Autumn 1952 p. 191).

Chapter 2

1 Alan Garner in Finlayson 'Myths and Passages'.

2 The name is taken from the medieval story of 'Elidor and the Golden Ball' preserved by Giraldus Cambrensis, in which fairyland seems to be a symbol of lost innocence; when he chose the name, from K. M. Briggs *The Anatomy of Puck* (p. 42 'Every now and then we catch a glimpse of the beautiful and harmless country of Elidor's fairies') Garner misunderstood it to be a synonym for fairyland rather than a personal name.

3 As a number of critics have noted, Roland is 'Thursday's child' and thus has 'far to go'. It is on a Thursday that Roland first sees the two men from Elidor in the garden.

4 Alan Garner, interviewed by the author 9 Feb 1979.

5 'The Door in the Wall' can be seen as a story about the rejection of the shaman/poet's call, one of the themes of Garner's most recent

play, *Strandloper*. It is a story of peculiar potency, and is obviously important to Garner. The Iron Gates are another version of the Door, 'which is not found by seeking', and Colin and Susan's ennui when they are excluded from Cadellin's world parallels that of Wells' Lionel Wallace. Thought of the garden behind the Door in the Wall conjures up in him 'the haunting memory of a beauty and a happiness that filled his heart with insatiable longings, that made all the interests and spectacle of worldly life seem dull and tedious and vain to him'.

6 *The Moon of Gomrath* chapter 20.

7 Malebron is the servant of Oberon (see H. A. Guerber *Myths and Legends of the Middle Ages* pp. 225 and 238). There is little significance in this: it is the first syllable of his name that is important.

8 Alan Garner 'Who, How, Why'.

9 See H. C. N. Williams *Coventry Cathedral* p. 7.

10 Garner retains the names of the four ´cities, but not the traditional identifications of treasure and city. Malebron gives Roland 'the Spear of Ildana from Gorias' not Finias (or Findias here) as one might expect. The stone of Fal is widely equated with the stone of Scone.

11 See Paul Hudson *The Devil's Picturebook* (London, 1972) chapter 2: 'It is possible that the four tarot suits refer to the four castes of Hinduism: the cup to the priests of Brahmins, the sword to the warrior overlords or Kshatriyas, the coin to the merchants or Vaisyas, and the baton to the serfs or Sudras.'

12 O'Grady *Silva Gadelica* p. 409.

13 Bromwich *Trioedd Ynys Prydein* appendix 3 p, 241. It is from this list that Garner, and Lloyd Alexander in his *The Book of Three* took the sword name Dyrnwyn.

14 Graves *The White Goddess* chapter 6.

15 'Child Waters', Child *The English and Scottish Popular Ballads* no. 63.

16 Indeed, we are told that at the song of Findhorn 'Streams danced, and rivers were set free'.

17 David Jones 'Sherthursdaye and Venus Day', *Anathémata* p. 224.

18 See Michael Archer *Stained Glass* p. 31.

19 See K. M. Briggs *A Dictionary of British Folk-Tales* A.1 p. 180; J. Jacobs 'Childe Rowland'; J. Jacobs *English Fairy Tales* pp. 117–24, 240–7 and frontispiece; R. Jamieson 'Popular Heroic and Romantic

Ballads etc.' in *Illustrations of Northern Antiquities etc* pp. 398–403.

20 See H. D'Arbois de Jubainville *The Irish Mythological Cycle and Celtic Mythology* chapter 14.

21 See Harry Price *Poltergeist Over England* p. 335.

22 See Dingwall, Goldney and Hall *The Haunting of Borley Rectory*, especially plate 5.

23 They are nos. 9970, 10283 and 10299, to be found in Briquet's third volume. They are slightly adapted to achieve the necessary continuous line.

Chapter 3

1 These words deliberately recall the mysterious trio of naked hanged men Ingcel sees in Da Derga's Hostel: 'Those are the three that are slaughtered at every time.'

2 See E. Cameron '*The Owl Service*: A Study'. She writes that 'Only Gwyn seems capable of passion in the large sense'. See also J. R. Townsend *A Sounding of Storytellers* pp. 86–8.

3 Alan Garner 'Inner Time'.

4 Myth seems a good shorthand word to use for 'Math ap Mathonwy' here, but in fact the story's origins as myth are buried beneath a number of literary and romantic accretions, and like the other stories in *The Mabinogion* its original form and meaning have been much confused.

5 Significantly, this occurs after Roger has been swimming. The posture in which Lleu can be killed requires him to make 'a bath for me on a river bank . . . and bringing a he-goat . . . and setting it beside the tub, and myself placing one foot on the back of the he-goat and the other on the edge of the tub' (G. & T. Jones *The Mabinogion* p. 70).

6 Llaw Gyffes means 'skilful hand'.

7 Graves *The White Goddess* chapter 18. All the names are chosen with great care. Roger, as Tony Watkins points out (in 'Writers for Children: Alan Garner'), means 'fame-spear'. Alison is a flower name.

8 Gronw is by no means always a villain in Welsh tradition: in Dafydd ap Gwilym's 'Achau y Dyllvan' Blodeuwedd, as an owl, laments him as 'soleil eclatant d'une race brilliante, Goronwy, le jeune homme vigoureux, le seigneur de Pennlyn, le beau, le grand'. See Loth *Les Mabinogion* vol. 1 p. 208 n. 2.

9 See Peter Plummer's contribution to *Filming The Owl Service*.

10 Alan Garner in J. Wintle and E. Fisher *The Pied Pipers*.

11 Alan Garner *The Hamish Hamilton Book of Goblins* p. 13.

Chapter 4

1 For a discussion of this see Stith Thompson *The Folktale* pp. 23–32.

Chapter 5

1 See Michael Hardcastle 'A Profile of Alan Garner' and Michael Moynihan 'Dark Dreams at Toad Hall'. My quotation is from Hardcastle.

2 Bob Dixon *'Catching Them Young 2: Political Ideas in Children's Fiction* (London, 1977) chapter 4; Elizabeth Cook *The Ordinary and the Fabulous* (second ed. Cambridge, 1976) p. 159; M. Z. Bradley review of *Red Shift, Fantasiae* vol. 4 no. 8 Aug 1976; E. Blishen 'Ambiguous Triptych'; A. Chambers 'Letter from England: Literary Crossword Puzzle . . . Or Masterpiece?'; *Times Literary Supplement* 'To the Dark Tower'.

3 As Aidan Chambers, an admirer of the book, observes, '*Red Shift* could be said to be about hardly anything else but distressing emotional intensity' ('Letter from England: A Matter of Balance').

4 See *Red Shift* p. 84.

5 See for instance J. R. Townsend *Written for Children* p. 250.

6 For a discussion of the need to keep such finds wrapped and to touch them as little as possible see C. Blinkenberg *The Thunderweapon in Religion and Folklore.*

7 This repetition also recalls *Elidor* chapter 4: 'So we lived, and no strife between us.'

8 Macey says (p. 31) 'I am the one the moon's axe spares'.

9 'When I last saw the figure, particles of scarlet still clung to its dress', Rev. E. Hinchliffe *Barthomley* p. 33.

10 'By heck, they don't half shift. Yellow when they're coming, and red when they're going.'

11 For the identification of the heavens with a mill in myths from all over the world, and a consideration of the symbol's meaning, see Santillana and von Deckend *Hamlet's Mill* passim. See also Rev. O. Cockayne *Leechdoms, Wortcunning, and Starcraft of Early England* vol. 3 'A Treatise on Astronomy and Cosmogony' p. 233: 'the heaven locketh up in its bosom all the world; and it turneth ever above us, swifter than any mill wheel.' Orion is *Smati-Osiris,* the Barley god, in the Egyptian Book of the Dead; R. H. Allen quotes from Hesiod *Works and Days* (*Star-Names and Their Meanings* p. 306):

> '*Forget not, when Orion first appears,*
> *To make your servants thresh the sacred ears;*'.

12 See L. Eckenstein *A Spell of Words* for a lengthy discussion of this relationship.

13 It should be noted that thunderstones were a talismanic cure for insanity and demoniacal possession. See Sir John Evans *The Ancient Stone Implements, Weapons and Ornaments, of Great Britain* chapter 5.

14 At the time of Hadrian Italy supplied only 0·9% of the Imperial Army. See G. Webster *The Roman Imperial Army* p. 108.

15 The Cornovii were also found in Caithness, the headland of the cats, and it seems likely that their name means something like 'the horned ones' or 'those with the pointed ears'. See Anne Ross *Pagan Celtic Britain* p. 143 and Richmond 'The Cornovii' p. 251. The Cats is certainly a possible name for a British tribe: there was a Clan Chattan to the east of Loch Ness, and the Catieuchlani, known to the Romans as Cassi, were a midlands tribe according to Ptolemy. See L. Eckenstein *A Spell of Words* part 1 chapter 1. The Brigantes were worshippers of the fertility goddess Brigid, as their name implies. Their dedications are to the 'matres'. T. C. Lethbridge (*Witches* chapter 8): 'One of the things one is compelled to notice when looking at the names of the Celtic tribes, whether the ancient ones of Gaul and Britain, or the more modern clans of Scotland, is that some of them are called after animals and others after the various names of the Great Goddess.' In the case of the Cats the identification with the traditional Cheshire Cat is clearly an added bonus.

16 Alan Garner 'Who, How, Why'.

17 Both Malbon's and Burghall's accounts are given in full in J. Hall (ed.) *Memorials of the Civil War in Cheshire*.

18 See J. Hall *Memorials of the Civil War in Cheshire* pp. 94–6. Also quoted by J. Hall *A History of the Town and Parish of Nantwich* pp. 158–9. This is the version of the massacre quoted in . . . *All Systems Go* . . . .

19 See Hinchliffe *Barthomley* p. 40, J. Hall *Memorials of the Civil War in Cheshire* p. 95.

20 John Vicars *Magnalia Dei Anglicana* vol. 2 p. 129.

21 See J. Partridge *An Historical Account of the Town and Parish of Nantwich* p. 66.

22 I cannot find any evidence to suggest that Byron was actually at the massacre, although it was undoubtedly his troops which were responsible. Those historians (for instance S. Gardiner *History of the Great Civil War 1642–1649*) who follow Vicars' *Parliamentary Chronicle* in declaring those in the church to have been par-

liamentary forces seem to be perpetuating a misunderstanding of Byron's supposed letter. R. N. Dore in *The Civil Wars in Cheshire* chapter 3 describes the massacred men as 'a small body of villagers under the Puritan schoolmaster, probably armed'.

23 See Jacqueline Simpson 'Fifty British Dragon Tales' and Egerton Leigh *Ballads and Legends of Cheshire* pp. 223–7.

24 See M. J. Hewitt *Medieval Cheshire* pp. 6, 156, 171.

25 I recognise that the use of the word 'shaman' here is unsatisfactory, and that it should properly be applied only to the ecstatic medicine men of 'primitive' tribes. However, although Eliade tells us that 'any ecstatic cannot be considered a shaman; the shaman specialises in a trance during which his soul is believed to leave his body and ascend to the sky or descend to the underworld' (*Shamanism* p. 5) and to talk of Garner's characters in this sense is impossible, the function of the shaman, to bring health and fertility to society by means of a ritualised re-experiencing of psychic or spiritual trauma, seems to me to have a bearing on Garner's work.

26 T. S. Eliot 'Little Gidding' 1, line 55.

27 St Paul II Cor. xii 2–3.

28 Marghanita Laski *Ecstasy: A Study of Some Secular and Religious Experiences* part 2 chapter 4. 'Intensity ecstasies' are contrasted with 'withdrawal ecstasies' in this most useful study. Laski characterises ecstasy as 'joyful, transitory, unexpected, rare, valued and extraordinary to the point of often seeming as if derived from a praeturnatural source' (part 1 chapter 1), a definition which for all its penetration does not quite fit my use of the word here. It seems to me that although she is correct to say that we would not naturally speak 'of a sad ecstasy, or of a trivial or worthless ecstasy' it is possible to speak of a terrible ecstasy. To speak of ecstasy as solely joyful seems out of balance. A 'terrible' ecstasy is not the same as the 'desolation' with which Laski contrasts ecstasy, but is rather the spiritual agony which is ecstasy's traditional opposite (an opposition which meets in extremes).

29 See Ted Hughes' famous interview with Egbert Faas for an interesting discussion of the artist as shaman. See also Alan Garner 'Inner Time'.

30 I. M. Lewis *Ecstatic Religion* chapter 7:3.

31 'Tam Lin' Child *The English and Scottish Popular Ballads* no. 39.

32 This episode of the German wine-grower strikes me as somewhat glib and forced; one regrets that Jan's 'betrayal' of Tom

were not slightly less melodramatic. As John Rowe Townsend writes (*A Sounding of Storytellers* p. 90), 'Her account of her previous brief affair with a married man is almost novelettish'.

33 C. Storr *Thursday* (London, 1971).

34 Alan Garner in Wintle and Fisher *The Pied Pipers* p. 234. *Seven Samurai* and *Throne of Blood* were made in 1954 and 1957 respectively by the great Japanese director Akira Kurosawa, whose most famous film, *Rashomon* (1950), pioneered the multiple narrative technique employed by Garner in the Thomas/Margery/John Fowler scene in the tower. Magoo, Face and Logan's madness is the result of ergot poisoning. Hugh MacDiarmid writes (in 'Plaited Like the Generations of Men' *Complete Poems* (London, 1978) vol. 2 p. 886)

'*When a woman grinds the corn with one hand*
Don't let it in your belly.'

35 The word 'roared' is used elsewhere in Garner's work in a similarly extended, almost metaphysical sense. See *The Moon of Gomrath* chapter 1, 'Trees roared high in the darkness'.

Chapter 6

1 Alan Garner 'A Librettist Speaks'. K. M. Briggs *A Dictionary of British Folk-Tales* has seven variants of this legend. The most important ones for *Potter Thompson* are 'Potter Thompson', 'King Arthur at Sewingshields' and 'The Wizard of Alderley Edge'.

2 Alan Garner 'A Librettist Speaks'.

3 For reviews of *Potter Thompson* see Hugo Cole in *The Listener* 29 May 1975; the *Guardian* 7 Jan 1975 and 23 June 1975; *The Times* 10 Jan 1975 and 24 June 1975; and the *Daily Telegraph* 10 Jan 1975.

4 Alan Garner and Gordon Crosse Programme note to *Potter Thompson*.

5 Alan Garner and Gordon Crosse Programme note to *Potter Thompson*.

Chapter 7

1 Alan Garner in *Children's Literature in Education* 'Alan Garner: Coming to Terms'.

2 Alan Garner in 'Living Language'.

3 Quoted in 'Living Language' from Robert's obituary in the local newspaper; the words are echoed in *Tom Fobble's Day*.

4 See the note to 'Happy Boz'll' in *The Guizer*: it is 'nothing but low language and povertiness'.

5 G. R. Levy *The Gate of Horn* p. 47. See also M. Eliade *Australian Religions* and *Birth and Rebirth*. Levy writes (p. 49) that 'impressed hands are common in Australia'. To lay one's hand on the wall is to claim right of entry: it is the equivalent of turning a key.

6 The temperance songs in *Granny Reardun* are, incidentally, taken from the book Roland finds in the church at the beginning of *Elidor*, Kirton's *Standard Temperance Reciter*. 'Dip your roll in your own pot at home' is about a stone-mason: just as Old William prefers a hymn which bears on his trade, so too does Robert in his ironic penchant for temperance hymns.

7 'Own' here should probably be understood as acknowledge rather than possess.

8 Alan Garner in Finlayson 'Myths and Passages'.

9 Alan Garner in Finlayson 'Myths and Passages'.

10 *The Moon of Gomrath* chapter 4.

11 Alan Garner in W. Foster 'A Feeling for Fantasy'.

12 Alan Garner in A. Chambers 'An Interview with Alan Garner'.

13 See *Sunday Telegraph* 'Man of Stones and Steeples'.

14 See Garner's linked essays 'The Edge of the Ceiling' and 'Aspects of a still life'.

15 Alan Garner in A. Chambers 'An Interview with Alan Garner'.

16 Brian Alderson 'A Wizard in his own Landscape'.

Chapter 8

1 See George Ewart Evans *Horse Power and Magic*.

2 D. Jones Preface to *In Parenthesis* (in *Epoch and Artist*).

3 M. Eliade *The Sacred and The Profane* p. 109.

4 Alan Garner 'Inner Time'.

5 Alan Garner *The Hamish Hamilton Book of Goblins*, introduction.

6 'We sacrificed the numinous for our other greatness – the intellect. The mistake has been to atrophy our dreams.' Alan Garner 'Inner Time'.

Bibliography

The bibliography is in three sections:

The writing of Alan Garner
A selection of the most important writing on Alan Garner
A select list of background reading which may illuminate Alan Garner's work.

The Writing of Alan Garner: PUBLISHED WORK

Books

The Weirdstone of Brisingamen. A Tale of Alderley Endpaper maps by Charles Green. Collins, London, 1960. p.b. (revised text) Puffin, Harmondsworth, 1963; Armada Lions, London, 1971. American edition Watts, New York, 1961, as *The weirdstone: a tale of Alderley*; Walck, New York, 1969 (1963 text); Collins World, New York, 1979 (1960 text). Translated as: *Feuerfrost und Kadellin* Benziger Verlag AG, Einsiedeln, 1963; *Brisingamen No Mahoh No Hoseki* Hyoron sha, Tokyo, 1969; *Den Förtrollade Stenen* Berghs, Malmö, 1974.

The Moon of Gomrath Endpaper maps by Charles Green. Collins, London, 1963. p.b. Puffin, Harmondsworth, 1965; Armada Lions, London, 1972. American edition Walck, New York, 1967; Collins World, New York, 1979. Translated as: *Gomrath No Tsuki* Hyoron sha, Tokyo, 1969; *Het Teken van Fohla* Lemniscaat, Rotterdam, 1970; *Månen over Gomrath* Branner og Korch, Copenhagen, 1975.

Elidor Illustrated by Charles Keeping. Collins, London, 1965. p.b. Puffin, Harmondsworth, 1967; Armada Lions, London, 1974. American edition (with textual alterations) Walck, New York, 1967;

(with English text) Collins World, New York, 1979. Translated as: *Elidor* Hyoron sha, Tokyo, 1969; *Elidor* Cecilie Dressler Verlag, Berlin, 1969; *Elidor det gyllene landet* Berghs, Malmö, 1971; *Elidor* Editorial Estela, Barcelona, 1971; *Elidor* Branner og Korch, Copenhagen, 1973; *Mustan Tornin Portilla* Werner Söderström, Helsinki, 1980.

Holly from the Bongs, A Nativity Play Photographs by Roger Hill, music by William Mayne. Collins, London, 1966.

The Old Man of Mow Photographs by Roger Hill. Collins, London, 1967. American edition Doubleday, New York, 1970.

The Owl Service Endpaper decorations by Griselda Greaves. Collins, London, 1967. p.b. Peacock, Harmondsworth, 1969; Armada Lions, London, 1973. American edition Walck, New York, 1968; Collins World, New York, 1979. Translated as: *Uglestellet* Branner og Korch, Copenhagen, 1969; *De tre fördömda* Berghs, Malmö, 1970; *Fukuroh Moyoh No Sara* Hyoron sha, Tokyo, 1972; *Det mystiske ugle-mønsteret* Gyldendal Norsk Forlag, Oslo, 1973; *Huuhkaja laakso* Werner Söderström, Helsinki, 1978.

The Hamish Hamilton Book of Goblins Edited by Alan Garner, illustrated by Krystyna Turska. Hamish Hamilton, London, 1969. p.b. Puffin, Harmondsworth, 1972, as *A Book of Goblins*. American edition Walck, New York, 1969, as *A Cavalcade of Goblins*.

Red Shift Collins, London, 1973. p.b. (with corrections) Lions, London, 1975; (3rd impression, with further corrections) Lions, 1977. American edition (with variant readings; this is Garner's preferred text) Macmillan, New York, 1973. Translated as: *Orion i ögat* Berghs, Malmö, 1973 (1st edition withdrawn from sale, as signatures incorrectly bound); *Rotverschiebung* Diederichs Verlag, Dusseldorf, 1980; Japanese translation to be published by Hyoron sha, Tokyo.

The Guizer: A Book of Fools With illustrations from V. Pritchard *English Medieval Graffiti*. Hamish Hamilton, London, 1975. p.b. (with revised introduction) Fontana Lions, London, 1980. American edition Morrow, New York, 1976.

The Stone Book Etchings by Michael Foreman. Collins, London, 1976. p.b. (with new illustrations by Michael Foreman) Lions, London, 1979. American edition (with publisher's preface and alterations) Collins World, New York, 1978. Swedish translation to be published by Sjöstrand, Vällingby. Norwegian translation to be published by Gyldendal Norsk Forlag, Oslo. Japanese translation to be published by Hyoron sha, Tokyo.

Tom Fobble's Day Etchings by Michael Foreman. Collins, London, 1977. p.b. (with new illustrations by Michael Foreman) Lions,

London, 1979. American edition (with publisher's preface and alterations) Collins World, New York, 1979. Swedish translation to be published by Sjöstrand, Vällingby. Norwegian translation to be published by Gyldendal Norsk Forlag, Oslo. Japanese translation to be published by Hyoron sha, Tokyo.

Granny Reardun Etchings by Michael Foreman. Collins, London, 1977. p.b. (with new illustrations by Michael Foreman) Lions, London, 1979. American edition (with publisher's preface and alterations) Collins World, New York, 1978. Swedish translation to be published by Sjöstrand, Vällingby. Norwegian translation to be published by Gyldendal Norsk Forlag, Oslo.

The Aimer Gate Etchings by Michael Foreman. Collins, London, 1978. p.b. (with new illustrations by Michael Foreman) Lions, London, 1979. American edition (with publisher's preface and alterations) Collins World, New York, 1979. Swedish translation to be published by Sjöstrand, Vällingby. Norwegian translation to be published by Gyldendal Norsk Forlag, Oslo.

The Girl of the Golden Gate; The Golden Brothers; The Princess and the Golden Mane; The Three Golden Heads of the Well All four illustrated by Michael Foreman. p.b. Collins, London, 1979. In one volume, with enlarged illustrations, as *Alan Garner's Fairytales of Gold*. Collins, London, 1980. American edition Philomel Books, New York, 1980. *The Golden Brothers* translated as *Deux Frères en Or, The Princess and the Golden Mane* translated as *La Princesse et la Crinière d'Or* Editions Gallimard, Paris, 1980.

The Lad of the Gad Collins, London, 1980. American edition (with revised introduction) Philomel Books, New York, 1981.

The Breadhorse Illustrated by Albin Trowski, Collins, London, 1975.

Libretti

Holly from the Bongs: A Nativity Opera Text by Alan Garner, music by Gordon Crosse. Oxford University Press, London. Performed 1974. Text differs from play version.

Potter Thompson Text by Alan Garner, music by Gordon Crosse. Oxford University Press, London. Performed 1975.

Uncollected short fiction and verses

'The Obelisk' *Ulula*, the Manchester Grammar School Magazine, Spring 1952.

'Mauldeth Road Station' *Ulula*, Summer 1952.

'The Star of Galgoid' *Time and Tide* 30 Nov 1961. Reprinted as 'Galgoid the Hewer' C. Hillier ed. *Winter's Tales for Children 2* (Macmillan, London, 1966).

'How Finn Maccumhail was in the House of the Rowan Tree without Power to Stand or Leave to Sit Down' W. Mayne ed. *The Hamish Hamilton Book of Heroes* (Hamish Hamilton, London, 1967).

'Feel Free' E. Blishen ed. *Miscellany 4* (Oxford University Press, London, 1967). Also in S. Dickinson ed. *The Restless Ghost* (Collins, London, 1970) and S. Dickinson ed. *Ghostly Experiences* (Armada Lions, London, 1972).

'In Case of Emergency' *Yorkshire Life* Christmas Review 1967.

'Carol' *Sunday Times* 21 Jan 1968.

'Small World' K. Webb ed. *The Friday Miracle and Other Stories* (Puffin, Harmondsworth, 1969).

'R.I.P.' *Sunday Times* 17 Jan 1971. Also in G. Greaves ed. *The Burning Thorn* (Hamish Hamilton, London, 1971) and G. Grigson ed. *Unrespectable Verse* (Allen Lane, London, 1971).

'Summer Solstice' G. Greaves ed. *The Burning Thorn*.

'The Bargest of Nidderdale' *PHP* (Peace, Happiness and Prosperity) (Tokyo) Dec. 1971.

'The Flying Childer' L. Garfield ed. *A Baker's Dozen* (Ward Lock, London, 1973).

'House by Jodrell' G. Greaves ed. *Alan Garner* (E. J. Morten, Manchester, 1973)

'Grid Reference' G. Greaves ed. *Alan Garner*.

'Development' *Cacophony,* the Magazine of Keele English Society, no. 1, Spring 1975.

'Solar System' *Cacophony* no. 1, Spring 1975.

'Rascally Tag' *Jubilee Jackanory* (BBC, London, 1977). This story differs textually from the version printed in *The Lad of the Gad*.

'The Island of the Strong Door', poem by Alan Garner, photographs by Paul Caponigro, *Aperture* no. 82, 1979.

Essays and Lectures

Judge's remarks, Puffin Club short story competition, *Puffin Post* vol. 1 no. 4, 1967.

'A Bit More Practice' *Times Literary Supplement* 6 June 1968. Reprinted in M. Meek, A. Warlow and G. Barton *The Cool Web: The Pattern of Children's Reading* (Bodley Head, London, 1977); reprinted in part in M. Crouch and A. Ellis *Chosen for Children* (3rd edition, The Library Association, London, 1977).

'Owl Service' *Ulula* Summer 1968.

Untitled contribution to A. Chambers *The Reluctant Reader* (Pergamon Press, Oxford, 1969) pp. 104–7.

'Introduction' E., A., and K. Garner *Filming The Owl Service* (Armada, London, 1970).

Untitled contribution to J. R. Townsend *A Sense of Story* (Longman Young Books, Harmondsworth, 1971) pp. 117-18.
'Creativity and Communication' *Tower Grange* (Bolton) 1972.
'Author's note' Programme, *Holly from the Bongs: A Nativity Opera* (Manchester Cathedral 9-14 Dec 1974).
Programme note (with Gordon Crosse), Programme, *Potter Thompson* (Church of Mary Magdalene, Munster Square, World Premiere 9 Jan 1975).
'A Librettist Speaks' *Music and Musicians* Jan 1975.
'Inner Time' P. Nicholls ed. *Science Fiction at Large* (Victor Gollancz, London, 1976); p.b. as *Explorations of the Marvellous* (Fontana, London, 1978).
'An Open Letter from Alan Garner to Peter Plummer' *School Bookshop News* 2, May 1975.
'When I was 10 I understood – and the fun went out of war' *TV Times* 11-17 Jan 1975.
'Who, How, Why' G. Greaves ed. *Alan Garner.*
'Minds that Matter' *School Bookshop News* 7, Summer 1977.
'Aspects of a still life' *The Listener* 15 Sept 1977.
'The Edge of the Ceiling' M. Dickens and R. Sutcliff eds. *Is Anyone There?* (Peacock, Harmondsworth, 1978).
Untitled extract from lecture 'The Fine Anger' *PN Review* 13, vol. 6 no. 5, 1979, 'Crisis for Cranmer & King James'.
'Alan Garner on Recording', sleeve note to *Tom Fobble's Day, read by the author* (Argo records ZDSW 727).
'The Stone Book Quartet' *Living Language,* BBC booklet to accompany radio programmes, Spring 1980.
'The Fine Anger' G. Fox and G. Hammond eds *Responses to Children's Literature: Proceedings of the Fourth Symposium of the International Research Society for Children's Literature, 1978* (K. G. Saur, New York, 1980).

Reviews

'Saving a masterpiece from a thousand years of language', review of G. Schmitt *The Heroic Deeds of Beowulf,* I. Serraillier *Beowulf the Warrior,* R. Sutcliff *Beowulf (Dragon-Slayer),* R. Nye *Bee Hunter. The Times* 6 July 1968.
'A Joy to Celebrate', review of G. Uden *A Dictionary of Chivalry. The Times* 9 Sept 1968.
'Real Mandrakes in Real Gardens', review of J. Gordon *The Giant Under the Snow,* R. E. Jackson The Poltergeist, J. L. Curry *Beneath the Hill,* M. Baker *The Mountain and the Summer Stars. New Statesman* 1 Nov 1968. Reprinted in part in V. Haviland *Children and Literature: Views and Reviews* (Bodley Head, London, 1974).

171

Untitled review of K. Crossley-Holland and J. Paton Walsh *Wordhoard: Anglo-Saxon Stories for Young People. The Times* 9 Aug 1969.
'Not in Front of the Adults', review of Iona and Peter Opie *Children's Games in Street and Playground. Guardian* 16 Oct 1969.
'Jacobs's joyous collection of British Folklore', review of J. Jacobs *Celtic Fairy Tales. The Times* 25 April 1970.
'The Death of Myth', review of L. Garfield and E. Blishen *The God Beneath the Sea. New Statesman* 6 Nov 1970; *Children's Literature in Education* 3, Nov 1970.
'Faery Teller', review of Maureen Duffy *The Erotic World of Faery. Guardian* 19 Oct 1972.

Other

'Magic' *Puffin Post* Birthday Edition, April 1966.
'Alan Garner has set a Puffin Riddle' *Puffin Post* vol. 1 no. 1, 1967.
'William Mayne U.F.O.' *Puffin Post* vol. 1 no. 3, 1967.
'. . . and now WRITE a STORY and WIN a visit to Brisingamen' *Puffin Post* vol. 1 no. 3, 1967.
'Short Story Competition' *Puffin Post* vol 1 no. 4, 1967.
Introduction to M. Laski 'The Tower' in *Author's Choice* (Hamish Hamilton, London, 1970).
G. Greaves ed. *Alan Garner* (Datapack Biographies no. 1, E. J. Morten, Manchester, 1973), an experimental publication which never went on general sale, contains an essay, 'Who, How, Why', two poems, 'House by Jodrell' and 'Grid Reference', a bibliography, reactions to the television adaptation of *The Owl Service* by an 'adult' and a 'schoolgirl', a number of photographs, and facsimile reproductions of pages of Alan Garner's memorabilia, mss. and notebooks, including the plan of Roland and Malebron's relationship I quote on p. 52, a page of the *Potter Thompson* score, a page of notes about flintlocks and matlocks for *Red Shift*, a page of the *Holly from the Bongs* ms. and a fascinating page of Celtic names and ogham characters noted for *The Weirdstone of Brisingamen*.
For important interviews, see bibliography p. 174, especially Chambers, A.; Children's Literature in Education; Finlayson, I.; Wintle, J.

UNPUBLISHED WORK: a selection

Libretti

'The Green Mist' 1971
'The Bellybag', music by Richard Morris, performed 1971

Film and TV scripts
'The Owl Service', in eight parts, Granada Television 1969
'Feel Free' 1974
'Red Shift' BBC 1978
'Lamaload' BBC 1979
'To Kill a King' BBC 1980
'Lurga Lom' 1980
'Writer's Workshop: Images' Thames Television 1980
'Strandloper' BBC 1981

Radio Plays
'Have You Met Our Tame Author?' BBC 1962
'Elidor' BBC 1962
'In Case of Emergency' 1964
'Thor and the Giants', two versions, BBC 1965 and 1979
'Loki and the Storm Giant', two versions, BBC 1965, as 'Idun and the Apples of Life', and 1979
'Baldur the Bright', two versions, BBC 1965 and 1979. The interim, 1974, versions of these three plays were adapted for radio by Paddy Bechely
'The Stone Book' BBC 1980
'Granny Reardun' BBC 1980
'The Aimer Gate' BBC 1980
'Tom Fobble's Day' BBC 1980

Radio Talks
'Four Hairy Herrings: A Short Survey of Nonsense', four programmes, BBC 1962
'Merlin's Isle', four programmes, BBC 1963
'My Delight' BBC 1978

Unpublished Lectures and Papers
'A Brief Summary of the Facts Concerning Two Important Timber-Framed Listed Buildings' 1972
'Moving Language' 1975
'Family Oral Tradition and Applied Archaeology in East Cheshire' 1977
'Porlock Prizes' 1979

Films on Alan Garner with scripts by him
'Alan Garner' Penguin Books 1968
'One Pair of Eyes: . . . All Systems Go . . .' BBC 1972

'Writer's Workshop: Places and Things' Thames Television 1978
'The Edge of the Ceiling' Granada Television 1980

Records

'*The Stone Book*, read by the author' Argo ZDSW 724, 1979
'*Granny Reardun*, read by the author' Argo ZDSW 725, 1979
'*The Aimer Gate*, read by the author' Argo ZDSW 726, 1979
'*Tom Fobble's Day*, read by the author', Argo ZDSW 727, 1979

Select List of interviews with, articles and essays on, reviews and critical considerations of Alan Garner and his writing

Works marked with an asterisk have not been seen

AERS, LESLEY 'Alan Garner: An Opinion', *Use of English* 22:2, Winter 1970
ALDERSON, BRIAN 'On Suffering the Prevalence of Trolls', *The Times* 26 June 1969, 'Writing an Onion', *The Times* 19 Sept 1973, 'A Wizard in his own Landscape', *The Times* 24 Aug 1977
BARTLE, F. R. *'Alan Garner', New South Wales *Children's Libraries Newsletter* 8, May 1972
BENTON, MICHAEL 'Detective Imagination', *Children's Literature in Education* 13, March 1974
BLISHEN, EDWARD 'Ambiguous Triptych', *Times Educational Supplement* 12 Oct 1973, 'Garner's Quartet', *Books and Bookmen* June 1971
BOLTON, P. G. 'Illness led Alan to a dazzling career', *Knutsford Guardian* 6 Dec 1979
BOOTH, MARTIN 'Marriage of Soul with Stone', *Times Educational Supplement* 20 Oct 1976
BREWER, ROSEMARY 'Alan Garner: A Perspective', *Orana* 14 (4) Nov 1978
BRYDEN, RONALD 'The Man Who Created "The Owl Service"', *Observer* Colour Magazine 25 Jan 1970, 'Out of the juvenile ghetto', *The Listener* 90, 8 Nov 1973
CAMERON, ELEANOR *The Green and Burning Tree: On the Writing and Enjoyment of Children's Books* (Boston, 1969). 'The Owl Service: A Study', *Wilson Library Bulletin* Dec 1969
CHAMBERS, AIDAN *The Reluctant Reader* (Oxford, 1969), 'Letter from England: Literary Crossword Puzzle . . . Or Masterpiece?' *Horn Book* Oct 1973, 'Letter from England: A Matter of Balance', *Horn Book* Aug 1977, 'An Interview with Alan Garner', *Signal* 27, Sept 1978, 'Letter from England: The Play's the Thing', *Horn Book*

April 1979, 'An Interview with Alan Garner', N. Chambers ed. *The Signal Approach to Children's Books* (London, 1980)

CHAMBERS, NANCY Review of *The Stone Book, Sunday Times* 5 Dec 1976

COOLEY, PAMELA 'Young Writer with a New Dimension', *Times Educational Supplement* 6 Oct 1967

Children's Literature in Education 'Alan Garner: Coming to Terms', *Children's Literature in Education* 1, March 1970

COLE, HUGO Review of *Potter Thompson, The Listener* 29 May 1975

County Express (Cheshire) 'Author faces facts 50 feet up tower', *County Express* 16 Dec 1974

CROSSE, GORDON '"Potter Thompson" – An Introduction', *Opera* vol. 26 no. 1, Jan 1975

CUMMING, JOHN 'Older Fiction', *Tablet* 15 Dec 1973

DENVER, GERALD & GREEN, ROBERT 'Alan Garner', *Fullerian '70*, Watford Grammar School 1970

DUNNE, COLIN 'The Compulsive Writer', *Daily Mirror* 21 Sept 1967

ELLIOTT, RALPH 'Moments of Awakening', *The Canberra Times* 21 Oct 1978, '"You Loomering, Gawming Kay-Pawed Gowf" and other delights', *The Canberra Times* 1 June 1980. See bibliography p. 181

ENRIGHT, D. J. 'Dynasties Pass', *Guardian* 25 Sept 1978

ESMONDE, MARGARET 'The External Primary Colours of Fantasy: The Use of Myth in the Novels of Alan Garner', *Fantasiae* vol. 2 no. 2, Feb 1974, 'Red Shift' *Fantasiae* vol. 2 no. 6, June 1974

FARLEY, JENNIFER 'Bardic Ring – Feminine Mystery', *Books and Bookmen* Dec 1967

FINLAYSON, IAIN 'Myths and Passages', *Books and Bookmen* Nov 1977

FISHER, MARGERY 'Magic for All Ages', *Sunday Times* 16 Sept 1973, 'Special Review: *Red Shift*', *Growing Point* vol. 12 no. 9, April 1974,'Special Review: *The Guizer*', *Growing Point* vol 14 no. 6, Jan 1976,'Special Review: Alan Garner *The Stone Book*', *Growing Point* vol. 15 no. 5, Nov 1976, 'Shaping a Man of Iron', *Sunday Times* 18 Dec 1977, 'Men of Stone: the end of a family saga', *Sunday Times* 10 Sept 1978

FOREMAN, MICHAEL 'Illustrating Garner', *School Bookshop News* Autumn 1979

FOSTER, WILLIAM 'A Feeling for Fantasy' *Scotsman* 22 Sept 1973

FOX, SUE 'The Writer Who Lives In His Own Never-Never Land', *TV Times* 3 Jan 1970

GARNER, ELLEN, GARNER, ADAM & GARNER, KATHARINE *Filming 'The Owl Service'* (with contributions by Alan Garner and Peter Plummer, London, 1970)

GILLIES, CAROLYN 'Possession and Structure in the novels of Alan Garner', *Children's Literature in Education* 18, Fall 1975

GILLIES, EVA 'The Timeless Fool', *Times Literary Supplement* 5 Dec 1975

GILLOTT, JACKY Review of *The Aimer Gate, The Times* 21 Sept 1978

GOODWIN, JUDI 'Moving House', *Manchester Evening News* 27 Dec 1975

GREEN, R. L. 'The Owl Hoots at Poulton', *Puffin Post* vol. 3 no. 3, 1969

HARDCASTLE, MICHAEL 'A Profile of Alan Garner', *Trade News* 19 Aug 1967, 'Why Alan Garner learnt (but didn't use) Welsh', *Liverpool Daily Post* 22 Aug 1967

HART, DENNIS 'Allen Garner', *The Elizabethan* March 1962

HAWORTH, BILL 'Meet Alan Garner . . . Under the Shadow of Jodrell Bank', *Stockport Advertiser* April 1975

HELLINGS, CAROL 'Alan Garner: His Use of Mythology and Dimensions in Time', *Orana* 15 (2) May 1979

HELSON, RAVENNA 'Through the Pages of Children's Books', *Psychology Today* Nov 1973

HOLLINDALE, PETER *Choosing Books for Children* (revised ed. London, 1975), 'Alan Garner's Magic', *Observer* 30 March 1975

HORRICKS, RAY 'With Alan Garner at Toad Hall and in London'. Sleeve note to Argo records ZDSW 724 and ZDSW 725 (*The Stone Book* and *Granny Reardun*)

JONES, C. & WAY, O. R. *British Children's Authors: Interviews at Home* (Chicago, 1976)

KEMBALL-COOK, JESSICA 'Correspondence (*Red Shift*)', *Children's Literature in Education* 15, Sept 1974, *'More on Alan Garner's *Red Shift*', *Fantasiae* 4 (11–12) Nov-Dec 1976

KLINGBERG, GÖTE *De Fremmede Verdener i børne -og ungdomsroman,* (Gyldendal, 1976)

KOHLER, MARGARET 'Author Study: Alan Garner', *Orana* vol. 16 no. 2, May 1980

LAVENDER, RALPH 'Truths of Childhood', *Times Educational Supplement* 29 Aug 1978

LEESON, BOB 'A Remembrance of Childhood', *Morning Star* 17 Nov 1979

LE GUIN, URSULA 'No, Virginia, there is not a Santa Claus', *Foundation* 6, 1974

MAHLQVIST, STEFAN *Article in De Oversatts for Ungdom (Lund, 1976), *'Hemma hos Alan Garner' På Stan. Veckan. 31 Dec 1976–7 Jan 1977

MANNING, ROSEMARY 'Manchester Mystery', *The Teacher* 26 Nov 1965

MAYNE, WILLIAM *The Big Egg* (London, 1967), 'Alan Garner', *Puffin Post* vol. 1 no. 3, 1967

MCVITTY, WALTER 'Chickenshit in New Children's Classic', *Nation Review* 8 Mar 1974, 'Compact Ideas in a limited space: An in-depth look at Alan Garner's *Red Shift*', *Reading Time* April 1974, *School Bookshop News* 10, Summer 1978, 'Alan Garner' in D. L. Kirkpatrick (ed.) *Twentieth Century Children's Writers* (London, 1978)

MEEK, MARGARET 'Reaching Below the Surface', *Times Literary Supplement* 2 Dec 1977, 'A View from the Steeple', *Times Literary Supplement* 29 Sept 1978

MOULD, G. H. 'The Weirdstone of Brisingamen: A Four-Way Experience', *School Librarian* vol. 15 no. 2, July 1967

MOYNIHAN, MICHAEL 'Dark Dreams at Toad Hall', *Sunday Times* 22 Dec 1968

PAVORD, ANNA 'How Graffiti Set Alan Garner Writing', *Observer* 16 Dec 1973

PEARCE, PHILIPPA 'The Owl Service', *Children's Book News* July/Aug 1967; also in M. Meek *et al. The Cool Web* (London, 1977)

PHILIP, NEIL 'Faery Lands', *Times Educational Supplement* 23 Nov 1979, 'Muted Revelations', *Times Educational Supplement* 28 Dec 1979, 'The Function of Myth in Children's Literature', *Tract* 29/30, 1980, 'Aspects of Myth and Folklore in Children's Fiction: with particular reference to contemporary writers', Ph.D. thesis, University of London, 1980

PLUMMER, PETER Untitled article, *School Bookshop News*, 1, Nov 1974; untitled article in R. Davis (comp.) *I've Seen a Ghost – True Stories from Show Business* (London, 1979). See Garner, Ellen

Puffin Post 'Garner Country', *Puffin Post* vol. 2 no. 2, 1968

QUIGLY, ISABEL 'The View from Mow Cop', *New Statesman* 9 Nov 1973

REES, DAVID 'Alan Garner: Some Doubts', *Horn Book* June 1979

RICHARDSON, PATRICK 'The Best of Garner', *New Society* 30 May 1968

Stockport Advertiser 'Alan Garner: Climbing His Family Tree', *Stockport Advertiser* 16 Dec 1976

Sunday Telegraph 'Man of Stones and Steeples', *Sunday Telegraph* 24 Oct 1976, 'Childhood Re-run', *Sunday Telegraph* Colour Magazine 20 Aug 1978

THORNBER, ROBIN '"Thrutch up, missus" says the shepherd', *Guardian* 3 Dec 1974

Times Educational Supplement 'Author's Circus', *Times Educational Supplement* 9 April 1976

Times Literary Supplement 'Heirs of Tolkien, Nesbit and Carroll', *Times Literary Supplement* 9 Dec 1965, 'Alan Garner: Thursday's

Child Has Far To Go', *Times Literary Supplement* 30 Nov 1967, 'The Long Tradition' *Times Literary Supplement* 26 June 1969, 'To the Dark Tower', *Times Literary Supplement* 28 Sept 1973

TOWNSEND, JOHN ROWE *A Sense of Story* (Harmondsworth, 1971), 'Fantasy and Legend', *The Spectator Guide to the Children's Book Show*', Manchester, 18–24 Oct 1973, *Written for Children* (revised ed. Harmondsworth, 1974), *25 Years of British Children's Books* (London, 1977), *A Sounding of Storytellers* (Harmondsworth, 1979)

TUCKER, NICHOLAS 'The Stone Book Quartet', *Bookmark* Spring 1980

WALSH, ROBIN 'Alan Garner: A Study', *Orana* vol. 13 no. 2, May 1977

WATKINS, TONY 'Writers for Children – Alan Garner', *Use of English* vol. 21 no. 2, Winter 1969, 'Alan Garner's *Elidor*', *Children's Literature in Education* 7, March 1972, 'Alan Garner' in D. Butts (ed.) *Good Writers for Young Readers* (St Albans, 1977)

WESTALL, ROBERT 'How Real Do You Want Your Realism?', *Signal* 28, Jan 1979

WINTON, JOHN 'Read Mystification', *Cheshire Life* Nov 1973

Select Bibliography of Background Literature

AARNE, ANTTI *The Types of the Folktale* (translated and enlarged by Stith Thompson, 2nd revision, Helsinki, 1964)

ADAMS, MORLEY *In the Footsteps of Borrow and Fitzgerald* (London, 1914)

ADDY, SIDNEY OLDALL *Household Tales with other Traditional Remains collected in the Counties of York, Lincoln, Derby and Nottingham* (London and Sheffield, 1895)

ALDERLEY EDGE *Alderley Edge and its Neighbourhood* (by L. D. Stanley, Macclesfield, 1843), *Alderley Edge: A Guide* (Manchester, 1863), *Alderley Edge Urban District, The Official Guide* (Alderley Edge, 1958)

ALLEN, R. H. *Star-names and their Meanings* (New York and London, 1899)

ALPERS, ANTONY *Legends of the South Sea* (London, 1970)

ANDREW, M. & WALDRON, R. *The Poems of the Pearl Manuscript* (London, 1978)

ARBOIS DE JUBAINVILLE, H. D. *The Irish Mythological Cycle and Celtic Mythology* (translated with additional notes by Richard Irvine Best, Dublin, 1903)

ARCHER, MICHAEL *Stained Glass* (London, 1979)

AUBREY, JOHN *Three Prose Works* (*Miscellanies, Remaines of*

Gentilisme and Judaisme and *Observations*, ed. J. Buchanan-Brown, Fontwell, Sussex, 1972)

AUDEN, W. H. & TAYLOR, P. B. *The Elder Edda: A Selection* (London, 1969)

AXON, W. E. A. *Cheshire Gleanings* (Manchester and London, 1884), *Nixon's Cheshire Prophecies* (Manchester and London, 1873)

BALFOUR, Mrs M. C. 'Legends of the Lincolnshire Cars', *Folklore* 2, June, September and December 1891.

BERGER, JOHN 'Writing a love scene', *New Society* 28 Nov 1968

BLEEK, W. H. I. and LLOYD, C. C. *Specimens of Bushman Folklore* (London, 1911)

BLINKENBERG, C. *The Thunderweapon in Religion and Folklore* (Cambridge, 1911)

BRIGGS, K. M. *The Anatomy of Puck* (London, 1959), *A Dictionary of British Folk-Tales in the English Language, incorporating the F. J. Norton Collection* (London, 1970–1), *A Dictionary of Fairies* (London, 1976)

BRIQUET, C. M. *Les Filigranes. Dictionnaire Historique des Marques du Papier, dès leur apparition vers 1282 jusqu'en 1600, avec 39 figures dans la texte et 16,112 fac-similés de filigranes* (Geneva, 1907)

BRITTEN, BENJAMIN *War Requiem*, Opus 66. (Disc, Decca Stereo Set 252/3, Preface by William Plomer, Commentary by John Culshaw)

BORROW, G. *The Bible in Spain* (London, 1843), *Romano Lavo-Lil: Word-Book of the Romany* (London, 1888)

BROMWICH, RACHEL *Trioedd Ynys Prydein. The Welsh Triads* (Cardiff, 1961)

BROWN, A. C. L. *The Origin of the Grail Legend* (Cambridge, Mass., 1943)

BROWN, DEE *Bury My Heart at Wounded Knee: An Indian History of the American West* (London, 1971)

BRIFFAULT, R. *The Mothers* (abridged with an introduction by Gordon Rattray Taylor, London, 1959)

BUTTERWORTH, Rev. J. R. *Saint Bertoline's* (Barthomley, 1965)

CAMPBELL, J. F. *Popular Tales of the West Highlands* (Paisley and London, 1890)

CAMPBELL, J. G. *The Fians* (A. Campbell (ed.) *Waifs and Strays of Celtic Tradition*, Argyllshire Series, no. 4, London, 1891)

CARLON, C. J. *The Alderley Edge Mines* (Altrincham, 1979)

CARMICHAEL, A. *Carmina Gadelica* (Edinburgh, 1900; enlarged ed. Edinburgh, 1929)

CARROLL, LEWIS *The Complete Works of Lewis Carroll* (London, 1939) pp. 1156–7

CHADWICK, NORA K. *Celtic Britain* (London, 1963), *The Celts* (Harmondsworth, 1970)

CHADWICK, NORA K. and DILLON, MYLES *The Celtic Realms* (London, 1967)

CHAMBERS, E. K. *The English Folk-Play* Oxford, 1933)

CHAMBERS, R. *Popular Rhymes of Scotland* (New edition, London and Edinburgh, 1870)

CHAMBERS, R. W. *Widsith: A Study in Old English Heroic Legend* (Cambridge, 1912)

CHILD, F. J. *The English and Scottish Popular Ballads* (Boston, 1882–98)

CHETHAM SOCIETY *Remains Historical and Literary Connected With the Palatine Counties of Lancaster and Chester* (vol. 2, Manchester, 1844)

CLOUSTON, W. A. *The Book of Noodles: Stories of Simpletons; or fools and their frolics* (London, 1888)

COCKAYNE, Rev. O. (ed.) *Leechdoms, Wortcunning, and Starcraft of Early England* (London, 1864–66)

COOMARASWAMY, A. K. and SISTER NIVEDITA *Myths of the Hindus and Buddhists* (London, 1913)

COSTER, CHARLES DE *Flemish Legends* (translated Harold Taylor, London, 1920)

COWARD, T. A. *Picturesque Cheshire* (London and Manchester, 1903)

CROSS, T. PEETE *Motif-Index of Early Irish Literature* (Bloomington, Indiana, 1952)

DALZIEL, MARGARET (ed.) *Myth and the Modern Imagination* (Dunedin, New Zealand, 1967)

DARLINGTON, THOMAS *The Folk-Speech of South Cheshire* (London, 1887)

DAVIDSON, H. R. ELLIS *Gods and Myths of Northern Europe* (Harmondsworth, 1964)

DAVIS, F. HADLAND *Myths and Legends of Japan* (London, 1912)

DENHAM, MICHAEL AISLABIE *The Denham Tracts* (ed. Dr James Hardy, London, 1892–5)

DENNETT, R. E. *Notes on the Folklore of the Fjort* (London, 1898)

DEREN, MAYA *Divine Horsemen* (London, 1953)

DEXTER, T. F. G. *Fire-Worship in Britain* (London, 1931)

DINGWALL, E. J., GOLDNEY, K. M. & HALL, T. H. *The Haunting of Borley Rectory* (London, 1956)

DODGSON, J. McN. *The Place-Names of Cheshire, Part 1* (Cambridge, 1970)

DORE, R. N. *The Civil Wars in Cheshire* Chester, 1966)

DUNDES, ALAN (ed.) *The Study of Folklore* (Englewood Cliffs, New Jersey, 1965)

DUNNE, J. W. *An Experiment with Time* (London, 1927)

DUTT, W. A. *Highways and Byways in East Anglia* (London, 1901)

EARWAKER, J. P. *East Cheshire: Past and Present; or A History of the Hundred of Macclesfield in the County Palatine of Chester* (London, 1877)

EBBUTT, M. I. *Hero-Myths and Legends of the British Race* (London, 1910)

ECKENSTEIN, L. *A Spell of Words: Studies in Language Bearing on Custom* (London, 1932)

ELIADE, M. *The Myth of the Eternal Return* (London, 1955), *Patterns in Comparative Religion* (London and New York, 1958), *Birth and Rebirth: The Religious Meanings of Initiation in Human Culture* (New York, 1958), *Myths, Dreams, and Mysteries* (London, 1960), *Shamanism: Archaic Techniques of Ecstasy* (revised and enlarged, London, 1964), *Myth and Reality* (London, 1964), *The Two and the One* (London, 1965), *The Quest: History and Meaning in Religion* (Chicago and London, 1969), *The Sacred and the Profane* (New York, 1961), *Australian Religions: An Introduction* (Ithaca and London, 1973)

ELLIOTT, RALPH 'Staffordshire and Cheshire Landscapes in *Sir Gawain and the Green Knight*' *North Staffordshire Journal of Field Studies* vol. 17, 1977, 'Hills and Valleys in the "Gawain" Country' *Leeds Studies in English* New Series vol. X, 1978, 'Woods and Forests in the "Gawain" Country' *Neuphilologische Mitteilungen* 1/LXXX, 1979

EVANS. GEORGE EWART *Ask the Fellows Who Cut the Hay* (London, 1956), *Horse Power and Magic* (London, 1979)

EVANS, GEORGE EWART & THOMSON, DAVID *The Leaping Hare* (London, 1974)

EVANS, SIR JOHN *The Ancient Stone Implements, Weapons and Ornaments, of Great Britain* (second ed., revised, London, 1897)

FAAS, EGBERT 'Ted Hughes and Crow: An Interview with Egbert Faas' *The London Magazine* Jan 1971

FORDHAM, FRIEDA *An Introduction to Jung's Psychology* (revised ed., Harmondsworth, 1959)

FOSTER, I. Ll. & ADCOCK, L. *Culture and Environment: Essays in Honour of Sir Cyril Fox* (London, 1963)

FOWLES, JOHN *Daniel Martin* (London, 1977)

FRANZ, M-L. VON *Shadow and Evil in Fairytales* (Zurich, 1974). See Jung, Emma

FRASER, J. T. *The Voices of Time: A Cooperative Survey of Man's Views of Time as Expressed by the Sciences and by the Humanities* (New York, 1966)

FRAZER, J. G. *The Golden Bough* (abridged ed., London, 1922)

GARDINER, S. *History of the Great Civil War 1642–1649* (second ed., London, 1910)

GENNEP, ARNOLD VAN *The Rites of Passage* (London, 1960)

GERALD OF WALES (GIRALDUS CAMBRENSIS) *The Journey Through Wales* and *The Description of Wales* (Harmondsworth, 1978)
GOLLANCZ, I. (ed.) *The Percy Folio* (London, 1905–10)
GRAVES, ROBERT *The Greek Myths* (Harmondsworth, 1955), *The White Goddess: An Historical Grammar of Poetic Myth* (London, 1948; amended and enlarged 1961)
GREGORY, LADY AUGUSTA *Cuchulain of Muirthemne* (fifth ed., Gerrards Cross, 1970), *Gods and Fighting Men* (second ed., Gerrards Cross, 1970)
GRINSELL, L. V. *The Folklore of Prehistoric Sites in Britain* (Newton Abbot, 1976)
GROOME, FRANCES HINDE *In Gipsy Tents* (Edinburgh, 1880), *Gypsy Folk Tales* (London, 1899)
GRUFFYD, W. J. *Math vab Mathonwy* (Cardiff, 1928)
GUERBER, H. A. *The Myths of Greece and Rome* (London, 1907), *Myths of the Norsemen from the Eddas and Sagas* (London, 1908), *Myths and Legends of the Middle Ages* (London, 1909)
GUEST, LADY C. E. *The Mabinogion* (London, 1849)
HALIFAX, JOAN *Shamanic Voices* (Harmondsworth, 1979)
HALL, J. *A History of the Town and Parish of Nantwich* (first ed. 1883, reprinted Manchester, 1972), (ed.) *Memorials of the Civil War in Cheshire and adjacent counties by Thomas Malbon, of Nantwich, Gent., and Providence Improved by Edward Burghall, Vicar of Acton, near Nantwich.* (The Record Society for the Publication of Original Documents Relating to Lancashire and Cheshire vol. xix, Manchester, 1889.
HALLIWELL, J. O. *Illustrations of the Fairy Mythology of A Midsummer Night's Dream* (London, 1845), *Popular Rhymes and Nursery Tales of England* (London, 1849)
HAVILAND, VIRGINIA (ed.) *Children's Literature: A Guide to Reference Sources* (Library of Congress, Washington, 1966; first supplement 1972; second supplement, with M. N. Coughlan, 1977)
HEARN, LAFCADIO *Kwaidan: Stories of Strange Things* (London, 1904)
HELM, ALEX *Five Mumming Plays for Schools* (London, 1969), *Cheshire Folk Drama* (Ibstock, Leicestershire, 1968)
HENDERSON, W. *Notes on the Folk-Lore of the Northern Counties of England and the Borders* (second ed., London, 1879)
HEWITT, M. J. *Medieval Cheshire* (Manchester, 1929)
HILL, GEOFFREY *Mercian Hymns* (London, 1971)
HINCHLIFFE, Rev. E. *Barthomley: In Letters From A Former Rector To His Eldest Son* (London, 1856)
HOLE, C. *Traditions and Customs of Cheshire* (London, 1937)
HOLLAND, ROBERT *A Glossary of Words Used in the County of Chester* (London, 1886)

HONE, WILLIAM *Ancient Mysteries Described* (London, 1823), *The Table Book* (London, 1827), *The Year Book* (London, 1864), *The Every-Day Book* (London, 1864)

HORROCKS, Rev. O. *St. Bertoline's* (Barthomley, 1972)

HOWEY, M. OLDFIELD *The Horse in Magic and Myth* (London, 1923)

HUGHES, TED 'Myth and Education', *Children's Literature in Education* 1, March 1970, *Crow: from the life and songs of the crow* (London, 1970; 2nd ed. 1972), 'Myth and Education', in Fox, G. and others (ed.) *Writers, Critics and Children* (London, 1976). See Faas, Egbert

HYDE, DOUGLAS (ed.) *The Lad of the Ferule. The Adventure of the Children of the King of Norway* (Irish Texts Society vol. 1, London, 1899)

JACKSON, K. H. *The International Popular Tale and Early Welsh Tradition* (Cardiff, 1961; The Gregynog Lectures). *A Celtic Miscellany* (revised ed., Harmondsworth, 1971)

JACOBS, JOSEPH *English Fairy Tales* (London, 1890), 'Childe Rowland', *Folk-Lore* 2 (June 1891), *Celtic Fairy Tales* (London, 1891), *More English Fairy Tales* (London, 1892), *More Celtic Fairy Tales* (London, 1894)

JACOBS, M. & GREENWAY, J. (comp. and ed.) *The Anthropologist Looks at Myth* (Austin, Texas and London, 1966)

JAMES, WILLIAM *The Varieties of Religious Experience* (37th impression, London, 1929)

JAMIESON, R. *Popular Ballads and Songs, from Traditions, Manuscripts, and Scarce Editions; with translations of similar pieces from the ancient Danish language, and a few originals by the editor* (Edinburgh, 1806), 'Popular Heroic and Romantic Ballads, translated from the Northern Languages, with Notes and Illustrations', in *Illustrations of Northern Antiquities, from the earlier Teutonic and Scandinavian Romances,* etc. (Edinburgh, 1814)

JENKINS, J. G. *Traditional Country Craftsmen* (revised ed. London, 1978)

JONES, DAVID *Anathémata* (London, 1952), *Epoch and Artist* (London, 1959)

JONES, EDMUND *A Relation of Apparitions of Spirits, In the County of Monmouth, and the Principality of Wales: with other notable relations from England; together with observations about them: designed to confute and to prevent the infidelity of denying the being and Apparition of Spirits; which Tends to Irreligion and Atheism* (Newport, 1813)

JONES, GWYN & JONES, THOMAS *The Mabinogion* (London, 1949)

JUNG, C. G. *The Collected Works of C. G. Jung* ed. H. Read, M. Fordham, G. Adler, tr. R. F. C. Hull (London, 1953–00); especially vols. 5, 8, 9:1, and 9:2, *Memories, Dreams, Reflections* (recorded and edited by Aniela Jaffé, London, 1963)

JUNG, EMMA & FRANZ, M. L. VON *The Grail Legend* (London, 1971)

KIRK, ROBERT *The Secret Common-Wealth* (ed. S. F. Sanderson, Cambridge, 1976)

KIRTON, J. W. *Standard Temperance Reciter* (London, 1877)

LASKI, MARGHANITA *Ecstasy: A Study of some Secular and Religious Experiences* (London, 1961)

LEACH, MARIA (ed.) *Funk and Wagnall's Standard Dictionary of Folklore, Mythology and Legend* (London, 1975)

LEGH, GERARD *The Accedens of Armorye* (first pub. 1562; second edition, London, 1568)

LEIGH, EGERTON *Ballads and Legends of Cheshire* (London, 1867), *A Glossary of Words Used in the Dialect of Cheshire, founded on a similar attempt by Roger Wilbrahim, F.R.S. and F.S.A., Contributed to the Society of Antiquaries in 1817* (London and Chester, 1877)

LETHBRIDGE, T. C. *Gogmagog: The Buried Gods* (London, 1957), *Witches: Investigating an Ancient Religion* (London, 1962)

LEVY, G. R. *The Gate of Horn* (London, 1948)

LEWIS, I. M. *Ecstatic Religion* (Harmondsworth, 1971)

LIGHTFOOT, Dr JOHN *A Few, and New Observations, upon the Booke of Genesis. The most of them certaine, the rest probable, all harmlesse, strange & rarely heard off before* (London, 1642)

LOOMIS, R. S. *Celtic Myth and Arthurian Romance* (New York, 1926), *Wales and the Arthurian Legend* (Cardiff, 1956), (ed.) *Arthurian Literature in the Middle Ages* (Oxford, 1959), *The Grail: From Celtic Myth to Christian Symbol* (Cardiff and New York, 1963)

LOTH, J. *Les Mabinogion* (second ed., Paris, 1913)

LUOMALA, KATHARINE 'Numskull Clans and Tales: Their Structure and Function in Oceanic Asymmetrical Joking Relationships' in Jacobs and Greenway *The Anthropologist Looks at Myth*

LYSONS, DANIEL *Magna Brittanica* (vol. 2, part 2: *The County Palatine of Cheshire*, London, 1810; vol. in B.L. with numerous manuscript and other additions by Mathew Gregson *c.* 1823)

MacCULLOCH, EDGAR *Guernsey Folklore* (London, 1903)

MacDOUGALL, Rev. JAMES *Folk and Hero Tales* (*Waifs and Strays of Celtic Tradition* no. 3, London, 1891)

MacNEICE, LOUIS *The Dark Tower: and other radio scripts* (London, 1947)

McNEILL, F. MARIAN *The Silver Bough* (vol. 1, *Scottish Folk-Lore and Folk-Belief*, Glasgow, 1957)

MacNEILL, MÁIRE *The Festival of Lughnasa* (London, 1962)

MALORY, SIR THOMAS *Works* (ed. Vinaver, Oxford English Texts,

2nd ed. Oxford, 1967)

MARSTON, JOHN *The Plays of John Marston* (ed. H. Harvey Wood, Edinburgh and London, 1934)

MEYER, KUNO 'The Adventures of Nera' *Revue Celtique* vol. X, Paris, 1889, *The Voyage of Bran Son of Febal* (with an essay by Alfred Nutt, London, 1895–7)

MOBERLY, C. A. E. & JOURDAIN, E. F. *An Adventure* (first published under the names Elizabeth Morison and Francis Lamont, London, 1911)

MORGANWG, IOLO (EDWARD WILLIAMS) *Iolo Manuscripts. A Selection of Ancient Welsh Manuscripts in Prose and Verse* (Llandovery, 1848), *Barddas; or, a collection of original documents, illustrative of the theology, wisdom and usages of the Bardo-Druidic system of the isle of Britain* (ed. J. Williams ab Ithel, Llandovery and London, 1862)

MORRIS-JONES, SIR J. *Taliesin* (*Y Cymmrodor,* The Magazine of the Honourable Society of Cymmrodorion, vol. XXVIII, London, 1918)

MURRAY, MARGARET *The God of the Witches* (second ed., London, 1952)

NASH, D. W. *Taliesin* (London, 1858)

NEUMANN, ERICH *The Great Mother* (London, 1955)

NICOLAISEN, W. F. H. *Scottish Place-Names: Their Study and Significance* (London, 1976)

O'GRADY, STANDISH H. *Silva Gadelica* (London and Edinburgh, 1892)

ORDNANCE SURVEY *Merionethshire* (Sheets XXXV.10 and XXXV.14, 1: 2 500, Southampton, 1889), *Cheshire* (Sheets XXVIII.10 and XXVIII.13, 1: 2 500, Southampton, 1909), *The Potteries* (Sheet 118, 1: 50 000, Second Series, Southampton, 1979)

ORMEROD, G. *The History of the County Palatine and City of Chester* (London, 1819)

ORTON, H. *Survey of English Dialects (A): Introduction* (Leeds, 1962)

ORTON, H. & BARRY, M. V. *Survey of English Dialects (B): vol. 2 The West Midlands* parts 1 and 2 (Leeds 1969 and 1972), part 3, 1971

ORTON, H. SANDERSON, S. & WIDDOWSON, J. *The Linguistic Atlas of England* (London, 1978)

O'SULLIVAN, SEAN *Folktales of Ireland* (London, 1966)

PARTRIDGE, J. *An Historical Account of the Town and Parish of Nantwich: with a particular Relation of the Remarkable Siege it Sustained in the Grand Rebellion, in 1643* (Shrewsbury, 1774)

PATON, L. A. *Studies in the Fairy Mythology of Arthurian Romance* (second ed., New York, 1960)

PETROVICH, WOISLAV M. *Hero-Tales and Legends of the Serbians* (London, 1914)

PETRY, M. J. *Herne the Hunter: A Berkshire Legend* (Reading, 1972)

PLATO *The Republic* (tr. H. P. D. Lee, Harmondsworth, 1975)

PRICE, HARRY *Poltergeist over England* (London, 1956)

PRIESTLEY, J. B. *Man and Time* (London, 1964)

PRITCHARD, V. *English Medieval Graffiti* (Cambridge, 1967)

RADIN, PAUL *The World of Primitive Man* (London, New York and Toronto, 1953), *The Trickster: A Study in American Indian Mythology* (with commentaries by Karl Kerenyi and C. G. Jung, London, 1956)

RAINE, KATHLEEN *Defending Ancient Springs* (London, 1967)

RALEIGH, J. H. 'The English Novel and Three Kinds of Time', *Sewanee Review* 62, 1954.

RATTRAY, R. S. *Akan-Ashanti Folk-Tales* (Oxford, 1930)

READER'S DIGEST *Folklore, Myths, and Legends of Britain* (London, 1973)

REES, ALWYN & REES, BRINLEY *Celtic Heritage* (London, 1961)

RHYS, SIR JOHN *Studies in the Arthurian Legend* (Oxford, 1891)

RICHMOND, IAN A. 'The Cornovii' in Foster and Alcock *Culture and Environment*

ROBERTS, P. *The Cambrian Popular Antiquities; or, An Account of some Traditions, Customs and Superstitions of Wales with observations as to their origins, &c. &c.* (London, 1815)

ROBINSON, E. & SUMMERFIELD, G. (eds.) *John Clare: Selected Poems and Prose* (London, 1967)

ROEDER, CHARLES 'Prehistoric and Subsequent Mining at Alderley Edge, with a Sketch of the Archaeological Features of the Neighbourhood', *Lancashire and Cheshire Antiquarian Society Transactions* vol. 19, 1901

ROLLESTON, T. W. *Myths and Legends of the Celtic Race* (London, 1911)

ROSS, ANNE 'The Human Head in Insular Pagan Celtic Religion' *Proceedings of the Society of Antiquaries of Scotland* vol. XCI pp. 10–43, *Pagan Celtic Britain* (London, 1967), *Everyday Life of the Pagan Celts* (London, 1970)

RUTHVEN, K. K. *Myth* (London, 1976)

SANTILLANA, GIORGIO DE & DECHEND, HERTHA VON *Hamlet's Mill: An Essay on Myth and the Frame of Time* (Boston, 1969)

SHAFFER, PETER *The Royal Hunt of the Sun* (London, 1964)

SHEPHERD, ODELL *The Lore of the Unicorn* (London, 1930)

SIKES, WIRT *British Goblins* (London, 1880)

SIMPSON, JACQUELINE *Icelandic Folktales and Legends* (Berkely and Los Angeles, 1972), *The Folklore of the Welsh Border* (London, 1976), 'Fifty British Dragon Tales' *Folklore* 89:1, 1978

SKENE, W. F. *The Four Ancient Books of Wales* (Edinburgh, 1868)

SMITH, E. W. & DALE, A. M. *The Ila-Speaking Peoples of Northern Rhodesia* (London, 1920)

SMITH, J. GORDON *Ancient Tales and Folklore of Japan* (London, 1908)

SPENCE, J. L. T. C. (Lewis) *The Popol Vuh. The Mythic and Heroic Sagas of the Kichés of Central America* (London, 1908), *The Myths of Mexico and Peru* (London, 1913), *Myths and Legends of the North American Indians* (London, 1914), *The Myths of Ancient Egypt* (London, 1915), *Myths and Legends of Babylonia and Assyria* (London, 1916), *The Mysteries of Britain* (London, 1928)

STANLEY, EDWARD, D. D. *Addresses and Charges, with a Memoir, by his son Arthur Penrhyn Stanley, M.A.* (London, 1851)

STEPHENS, T. *The Literature of the Kymry* (Llandovery, 1849)

STERNBERG, THOMAS *The Dialect and Folklore of Northamptonshire* (London and Northampton, 1851)

STOKES, WHITLEY 'The Voyage of Maelduin' *Revue Celtique* IX, X, Paris, 1888–9, 'The Voyage of the Húi Corra' *Revue Celtique* XIV, Paris, 1893, *The Destruction of Da Derga's Hostel* (Paris, 1902)

STOREY, DAVID *Saville* (London, 1976)

STURLUSON, SNORRI *The Prose Edda* (tr. and ed. A. G. Brodeur, New York, 1916)

SYKES, E. *Everyman's Dictionary of Non-Classical Mythology* (London, 1952)

TENNYSON, A. *The Poems* (ed. C. Ricks, London, 1969)

THOMPSON, F. H. *Roman Cheshire* (Chester, 1965)

THOMPSON, STITH *The Folktale* (New York, 1946), *Motif-Index of Folk Literature* (revised and enlarged ed. Copenhagen, 1955–58)

TIDDY, R. J. E. *The Mummer's Play* (Oxford, 1923)

TOLKIEN, J. R. R. & GORDON, E. V. *Sir Gawain and the Green Knight* (second ed., revised by Norman Davis, Oxford, 1967)

TOULMIN, STEPHEN & GOODFIELD, JUNE *The Discovery of Time* (London, 1965)

TUCKETT, ANGELA *The Blacksmith's History* (London, 1974)

VAUDRIN, BILL *Tanaina Tales from Alaska* (Oklahoma, 1969)

VICARS, JOHN *Magnalia Dei Anglicana (Gods Arke Overtopping the Worlds Waves, Or The Third Part of the Parliamentary Chronicle)* (London, 1646)

VINCENZ, STANISLAW *On the High Uplands: Sagas, Songs, Tales and Legends of the Carpathians* (tr. H. C. Stevens, London, 1955)

WAITE, A. E. *The Book of Black Magic and of Pacts* (Privately printed, 1898)

WATKINS, ALFRED *The Old Straight Track* (London, 1925)

WEBBER, RONALD *The Village Blacksmith* (Newton Abbot, 1971)

WEBSTER, GRAHAM *The Roman Imperial Army of the First and*

Second Centuries A.D. (London, 1969), *The Cornovii* (London, 1975)

WELLESZ, EMMY (intro.) *An Islamic Book of Constellations* (Bodleian Picture Book no. 13, Oxford, 1965)

WELLS, H. G. 'The Door in the Wall' in *The Short Stories of H. G. Wells* (London, 1927)

WELSFORD, ENID *The Fool: His Social and Literary History* (London, 1935)

WENTZ, W. Y. EVANS *The Fairy-Faith in Celtic Countries* (Oxford, 1911), *The Tibetan Book of the Dead (Bardo Thodol)* (London, 1927)

WESTON, J. L. *The Legend of Sir Gawain* (London, 1897), *The Quest of the Holy Grail* (London, 1913), *From Ritual to Romance* (Cambridge, 1920)

WHITE, J. J. *Mythology in the Modern Novel* (Princeton, 1971)

WILBRAHIM, R. *An Attempt at a Glossary of Some Words Used in Cheshire* (London, 1820)

WILLEFORD, WILLIAM *The Fool and His Sceptre* (London, 1969)

WILLIAMS, H. C. N. *Coventry Cathedral* (London, 1966)

WILLIAMS, SIR IFOR *The Poems of Taliessin* (English version by J. E. Caerwyn Williams, Dublin, 1968)

WILLIAMS, EDWARD See Morganwg, Iolo

WITHYCOMBE, E. G. *The Oxford Dictionary of English Christian Names* (Oxford, 1945)

WRIGHT, JOSEPH *English Dialect Dictionary* (Oxford, 1898)

WYATT, A. J. *Beowulf* (new ed. revised R. W. Chambers, Cambridge, 1933)

Index